AMERICAN THIRD PARTIES
SINCE THE CIVIL WAR

GARLAND REFERENCE LIBRARY
OF SOCIAL SCIENCE
(VOL. 227)

AMERICAN THIRD PARTIES SINCE THE CIVIL WAR
An Annotated Bibliography

D. Stephen Rockwood
Cecelia Brown
Kenneth Eshleman
Deborah Shaffer

GARLAND PUBLISHING, INC. · NEW YORK & LONDON
1985

Library of Congress Cataloging in Publication Data

Rockwood, D. Stephen.
American third parties since the Civil War.

(Garland reference library of social science ;
vol. 227)
Includes index.
1. Third parties (United States politics)—History—
Bibliography.   2. United States—Politics and government
—1865–1900—Bibliography.   3. United States—Politics
and government—20th century—Bibliography.   I. Title.
II. Series: Garland reference library of social science ;
v. 227.
Z7164.P8R63   1985   016.324273′09   83-49298
[JK2261]
ISBN 0-8240-8970-7 (alk. paper)

Printed on acid-free, 250-year-life paper
Manufactured in the United States of America

CONTENTS

v

PREFACE

The authors intend this bibliography to serve as a starting point for scholars and students studying American third parties. To this purpose we have included a chapter on theoretical studies of third parties that is as comprehensive as we could make it. Our chapters on the various third parties vary in regard to comprehensitivity according to the degree in which bibliographic coverage already exists. Thus the chapter on Socialist parties includes only materials published since 1952 since Egbert and Parson's *Socialism and American Life* provides definitive coverage up to that point, and the chapter on Progressive parties includes only major sources since several bibliographies already cover the same ground.

In most areas we have followed the general rule of providing complete coverage of the book-length material available, while limiting our inclusion of periodical material to those items which we felt were of considerable importance. A major exception to this rule, however, occurs in the section dealing with the third-party movements of the last two decades. Here we have discovered a shortage of scholarly and book-length studies and have included many articles from popular periodical publications to provide a needed starting point for future scholars.

As the coordinating editor for this work I made the final decisions concerning which items were included or excluded. I am, therefore, solely responsible for any lapses in coverage and sins of either omission or commission. I am also responsible for all errors of fact.

I would like to express my thanks to my co-authors for their tireless efforts in researching and writing. I also owe a great debt to Ms. Ann Craft for the competent typing and indexing that turned a jumble of note cards into a finished manuscript. Finally, I thank Mount Saint Mary's College for the support to all of us while we worked on this project.

D. Stephen Rockwood
Emmitsburg, Maryland

American Third Parties
Since the Civil War

CHAPTER 1

THIRD PARTIES: THEORY AND PRACTICE

Third parties with significant political strength are comparatively rare in the United States. Only eleven different third parties have attracted as much as 6 per cent of the popular vote since 1828. While serious third parties rapidly decline or disappear, many small doctrinal parties continue to contest election after election with limited success.

Attempts to explain the lack of success of third parties have focused on institutional and cultural factors. Before 1960, institutional causes such as the single-member district, plurality electoral system, the national election of a single president, the direct primary and restrictive ballot access laws were frequently advanced by scholars as major causes of the dominance of elections by two major parties. More recent scholarship has emphasized the importance of an underlying social consensus on political democracy, individual rights, free enterprise and separation of church and state and relegated institutional explanations to a secondary position. An exception to this trend has been recent defenders of the electoral college system who see it as a strong support of the two-party system.

The role of third parties in the American political system is frequently said to include advocating new programs of political or economic reform, acting as "safety-valves" through which dissatisfied groups protest existing policies and serving as a stopping place for voters moving between the major parties.

Scholars disagree on the impact of third parties on public policy and elections. A commonly held view is that when a third party attracts a significant following, at least one of the major parties will try to modify its position, absorb the third party's followers and, if victorious, enact many of the proposals previously supported by the third party. Other scholars contend that interest groups and major party factions are more important in pushing new policies. Third parties may, by pulling votes unevenly from the major parties, swing presidential elections from one party to the other. Scholarly estimates of the frequency of such impact vary, with the highest being six elections.

Third parties between the Civil War and World War II --the Populists, the Socialists and the two Progressive parties--stood to the left of the major parties and appealed to farmers and workers with economic and political reform. Third

parties before the Civil War and after World War II, however,
arose around the issues of egalitarianism (Anti-Masons), and
the extension of slavery (Free Soil), immigration (American
or "Know-Nothing" party) and civil rights (American Independents). The latter two parties clearly adopted positions more
conservative than the major parties. In 1980, an independent
candidate from the political center won over 6 per cent of the
popular vote.

One reason for the continuing scholarly attention to
third parties, which is probably greater than they merit, may
be the frustration that ideologically-motivated writers feel
with the moderation, compromises and ambiguous stands of the
major parties.

PRIMARY SOURCE MATERIALS

1. Burnham, W. Dean. <u>Presidential Ballots 1836-1892</u>. Baltimore: Johns Hopkins, 1955. 956 pp.

Collects county-level election results for presidential elections. For 1860 and 1892, major third parties are listed separately. Seven descriptive chapters contain both little-known facts and conventional interpretations regarding Southern Democratic, Constitutional Union, and Populist parties.

2. Diamond, Robert A., ed. <u>Guide to U.S. Elections</u>. Washington: Congressional Quarterly, 1975. 1103 pp.

This convenient collection of election data presents in a separate section the vote totals and percentages by states for all minor party presidential candidates from 1824 to 1972. Presidential primary section records votes of LaFollette, Roosevelt, and Wallace when they were seeking major party nominations. Biographical section on candidates provides personal and career data.

3. Johnson, Donald B., comp. <u>National Party Platforms</u>. 2 vols. 6th rev. ed. Vol. 1, 1840-1956; Vol. 2, 1960-1976. Urbana: University of Illinois Press, 1978. 1035 pp.

The first edition of this series was compiled by Kirk H. Porter, in 1924. Five later editions compiled by Porter and Johnson were published from 1956 to 1973. Volumes contain platforms of major and minor parties. A supplement was published in 1982 which included Anderson's 1980 platform.

4. Petersen, Svend. <u>A Statistical History of the American Presidential Elections</u>. New York: Ungar, 1968. 250 pp.

Contains state-level totals and percentages for elections from 1789 to 1964.

5. <u>Presidential Elections Since 1789</u>. 2nd ed. Washington Congressional Quarterly, 1979. 192 pp.

Repeats election data presented in the more comprehensive <u>Guide to U.S. Elections</u>, item 2, but also includes 1976 primary and election results.

6.   Robinson, Edgar E. The Presidential Vote 1896 to 1932.
      Stanford: Stanford University Press, 1934. 403 pp.

      Compilation of presidential election returns by counties
for ten elections. For 1912 and 1924, the Progressive parties
are combined with smaller parties under an "other" category.
Totals for each party are listed at the state level.

7.   Scammon, Richard M., comp. and ed. America Votes: A
      Handbook of Contemporary American Election Statistics.
      Vols. 8 to 14. Washington: Congressional Quarterly,
      1970-1981. Alice V. Gillivray, co-editor, vols. 12-14.

      Major advantage of this series is county-level break-
down of the vote won by Wallace in 1968. Anderson's votes in
1980, unfortunately, are combined with small parties in an
"other" category at the county level. Ward and district-level
totals are available for five major cities.

8.   Schlesinger, Arthur M., Jr. History of American Presi-
      dential Elections, 1789-1968. 4 vols. New York:
      McGraw-Hill, 1971. 3959 pp.

      Different historians describe each presidential elec-
tion from 1789 to 1968. Especially useful because appendices
on each election include interesting primary source material
such as newspaper editorials, speeches and pamphlets along
with platforms and state-level election results.

9.   Supreme Court of the United States. United States Re-
      ports. Vol. 393 and subsequent vols. Washington:
      U.S. Government Printing Office, 1969 to present.

      Contains Supreme Court's written opinions in cases
where third parties have challenged state laws restricting
their ballot access. See especially Williams v. Rhodes, 393
U.S. 23 (1968) and Anderson v. Celebrezze, decided on April 19,
1983.

10.   Wynar, Lubomyr R., comp. American Political Parties: A
      Selective Guide to Parties and Movements of the 20th
      Century. Littleton, Colo. : Libraries Unlimited,
      1969. 427 pp.

      A partly annotated bibliography listing a wide range
of reference works, periodicals, newspapers, documents and
scholarly works which provide both general background and specific information on American political parties. Third parties

covered are States' Rights Party (Dixiecrats) 1948; Progressives
of 1912, 1924 and 1948; Socialists, American Independents,
Prohibition Party and, despite the title, nineteenth-century
movements such as the Anti-Masonic, Know-Nothing, Liberty,
Free Soil, Greenback and Populist parties.

SECONDARY SOURCES

11.   Agar, Herbert. The Price of Union. Boston: Houghton
      Mifflin, 1950. 750 pp.

      Advances the view that American leaders consciously
rejected divisive parties of principle in favor of socially
diverse, undogmatic parties following the conflicts among the
parties in the 1850's.

12.   Aherns, Gary, and Nancy Hauserman. "Fundamental Elec-
      tion Rights: Association, Voting and Candidacy."
      Valparaiso University Law Review 14 (1980): 465-95.

      Argues that Supreme Court decisions on ballot access
have shifted between protecting third-party candidates' rights
and state interests.

13.   Alexander, Herbert E. Financing Politics: Money, Elec-
      tions and Political Reform. Washington: Congressional
      Quarterly, 1976. 299 pp.

      Brief references to minor parties note that the Supreme
Court upheld contribution disclosure requirements for small
parties and that no third party qualified for federal funds
for their convention or general election campaign in 1976.

14.   Bell, Leslie. "Constraints on the Electoral Success of
      Minor Parties in the United States." Political Stud-
      ies 25 (March 1977): 103-109.

      Identifies restrictive ballot access laws as probably
the greatest barrier to third parties and warns against exag-
gerating the contributions of such parties to reform.

15.   Bennett, James D. Frederick Jackson Turner. Boston:
      Twayne, 1975. 138 pp.

      Summarizes Turner's frontier thesis and the views of
its critics and defenders. Thesis is often cited as a factor
contributing to the American consensus behind democracy and

individualism which helps support two parties.

16.   Best, Judith V. The Case Against Direct Election of the
      President: A Defense of the Electoral College. Ith-
      aca, N.Y.: Cornell University Press, 1975. 235 pp.

      Contends that the electoral college's winner-take-all
rule within states discourages third-party candidates while
the proposed direct election method with runoff would attract
more. Without citing any historical or comparative evidence,
she asserts that the United States has serious divisions, as
does any nation, which may produce more parties.

17.   Bickel, Alexander M. Reform and Continuity: The Elec-
      toral College, the Convention, and the Party System.
      New York: Harper and Row, 1971. 122 pp.

      Contends that two-party dominance would be unlikely to
survive without the electoral college. Bickel evaluates four
reform proposals other than direct vote. Later deadlines for
candidates who seek ballot position would increase their oppor-
tunity of working within major parties.

18.   Billington, Ray A. America's Frontier Heritage. New
      York: Holt, Rinehart and Winston, 1966. 310 pp.

      Moderate defense of Turner's thesis claims that fron-
tier states usually adopted the most democratic practices of
eastern states, saw equality as a real possibility and, therefore, helped shape the American consensus behind these concepts.

19.   Binkley, Wilfred E. American Political Parties: Their
      Natural History. 4th ed., enl. New York: Knopf,
      1965. 486 pp.

      Brief reference to third parties sees them as evidence
of the failure of major parties to placate dissident factions.

20.   Bone, Hugh A. American Politics and the Party System.
      3rd ed. New York: McGraw-Hill, 1965. 684 pp.

      Two-chapter treatment of the two-party system and minor
parties reflects changes occurring in scholarly thinking after
the author's second edition was published in 1955. He adds
social factors to the cause of two-partyism, becomes more
cautious in attributing policy impact and sees primaries leading to third-party decline.

21.   _____. "Small Parties Casualties of War?" National
        Municipal Review 32 (November, 1943): 524-9, 565.

      Attributes decline in third-party strength to restric-
tive state laws motivated by suspicions of alien influence.
Author recommends more lenient, uniform laws on ballot access
to preserve free expression and the reform impetus of minor
parties.

22.   Boorstin, Daniel J. The Genius of American Politics.
        Chicago: University of Chicago Press, 1953. 200 pp.

      Contends that Americans share common beliefs, however
vaguely defined, emerging from a unique historical experience
which is free from the sharp revolutionary conflicts of Europe.
Two moderate parties are made possible by the continuity and
lack of dogma identified by Boorstin.

23.   Burnham, Walter D. Critical Elections and the Main-
        springs of American Politics. New York: Wiley, 1964.
        302 pp.

      Contends that third-party protest movements, excluding
major party bolts, are associated with the initial stages of
partisan realignment.

24.   Campbell, Angus, Philip E. Converse, Warren E. Miller,
        and Donald E. Stokes. The American Voter: An Abridge-
        ment. New York: Wiley, 1964. 302 pp.

      Landmark study of American voting behavior in the
1950's includes chapter on agrarian political behavior.
Authors suggest that historically, farmers turned quickly to
third parties in hard times because they were isolated from
information and organized groups.

25.   Ceasar, James. Reforming the Reforms: A Critical Ana-
        lysis of the Presidential Selection Process. Cam-
        bridge, Mass.: Ballinger, 1982. 201 pp.

      Challenges assumption on third parties underlying post-
1968 democracy reforms of the presidential nomination system.
Major parties need not be completely open because third parties now enjoy easier access to the ballot and the public.

26.   Chambers, William N. "Party Development and the American
        Mainstream." The American Party Systems: Stages of
        Political Development. William N. Chambers and Walter
        D. Burnham, eds. New York: Oxford University Press,
        pp. 3-32.

        Stresses economic prosperity, minimal class division,
and the liberal consensus as more satisfactory explanations of
two-party dominance than institutional factors.

27.   Charlesworth, James C. "Is Our Two-Party System Natural?"
        The Annals of the American Academy of Political and
        Social Science (item 94): 1-9.

        Contends that the two-party system is not the product
of cultural or institutional factors, but the result of pragmatic leaders who realized that two socially diverse parties
were necessary to govern under a system which divides power.

28.   Clubb, Jerome M., William H. Flanigan, and Nancy H.
        Zingale. Partisan Realignment: Voters, Parties, and
        Government in American History. Vol. 108. Beverly
        Hills, Calif.: Sage Publications, 1980. 311 pp.

        Although the major purpose of the book is to improve
correlation analysis of state election percentages to identify
realigning elections, the authors also find that third parties
are the strongest when alignments are deteriorating and the
weakest during realigning eras.

29.   Cronin, Thomas E. "The Direct Vote and the Electoral
        College: The Case for Meshing Things Up." Presidential
        Studies Quarterly 9 (Spring 1979): 144-62.

        A former supporter of direct vote and a member of the
Twentieth Century Fund Task Force urges serious study of the
bonus plan (item 113) which would be less likely to encourage
a proliferation of candidates than the direct vote plan.

30.   Diamond, Martin. The Electoral College and the American
        Idea of Democracy. Washington: American Enterprise
        Institute, 1977. 22 pp.

        Expresses the view that the direct vote system would
encourage minor parties and makes the novel argument that sectional parties would also be strengthened.

31.   Douglas, Paul H. The Coming of a New Party. New York:
       McGraw-Hill, 1932. 236 pp.

       Appeals to progressives to reject the major parties in
favor of a new party of farmers, labor and Socialists. New
parties must avoid hastily-organized campaigns, unsupported by
local and state organizations. (Douglas later served three
terms in the Senate as a Democrat from Illinois.)

32.   Dunn, Delmar D. Financing Presidential Campaigns. Wash-
       ington: Brookings, 1972. 168 pp.

       Endorses the repeal of Section 315(a) of the Communi-
cations Act in presidential elections if minor parties receive
a fraction of major party media time and campaign subsidies if
they exceed five percent of the vote.

33.   Duverger, Maurice. Political Parties: Their Organization
       and Activity in the Modern State. 1954. Translated by
       Barbara and Robert North. Reprint. London: Methuen,
       1969. 439 pp.

       French political scientist claims that the single bal-
lot, plurality election system maintains the two-party system
while proportional representation stops any trend toward two-
party dominance.

34.   Einsiedel, E.F., and M. Jane Bibbee. "The Newsmagazines
       and Minority Candidates: Campaign '76." Journalism
       Quarterly, 56 (Spring 1979): 102-5.

       Review of major newsmagazine coverage of McCarthy's
independent candidacy in 1976 leads to the conclusion that minor candidates receive infrequent and negative treatment.

35.   Elden, James M., and David R. Schweitzer. "New Third
       Party Radicalism: The Case of the California Peace
       and Freedom Party." The Western Political Quarterly,
       24 (December, 1971): 761-74.

       Study of minor party activists finds them to be middle
class persons (e.g., teachers, social workers) who are unable
to solve social problems they encounter.

36.   Epstein, Leon D. Politics in Wisconsin. Madison: Uni-
       versity of Wisconsin Press, 1958. 218 pp.

       The conservatism of the major parties in the state led
to a rarity in American politics: an unstable three-party sys-

tem. National New Deal policies eventually attracted Progressives to the Democrats and restored two-party competition after
a ten-year period.

37. _____. Political Parties in Western Democracies.
     New York: Praeger, 1967. 374 pp.

     Excellent comparative study contends that the United
States, with its transient third parties, comes closest among
western democracies to the two-party model because of its presidential election method, the usual absence of uncompromisable
issues and early enfranchisement of male workers.

38. Ewing, Cortez A.M. Presidential Elections: From Abra-
     ham Lincoln to Franklin D. Roosevelt. Norman: Univer-
     sity of Oklahoma Press, 1940. 226 pp.

     Claims that minor parties educate the public on policy
innovations before the major parties adopt them. Author argues
that minor parties with distinctive sectional bases altered the
outcome of four elections.

39. Fellman, David. The Constitutional Right of Association.
     Chicago: University of Chicago Press, 1963. 110 pp.

     Provides background on state laws limiting allegedly
subversive parties. Discussion of court decisions needs to be
supplemented with more recent cases such as Communist party of
Indiana vs. Whitcomb, 414 U.S. 441 (1974).

40. Fine, Nathan. Labor and Farmer Parties in the United
     States, 1828-1928. 1928 reprint. New York: Russell
     and Russell, 1961. 445 pp.

     A very detailed, but admiring and uncritical, account
of farmer and labor parties with emphasis on socialist parties.
The Progressives of 1924 are viewed as a promising model for
future parties.

41. Greer, Thomas H. American Social Reform Movements: Their
     Pattern Since 1865. New York: Prentice-Hall, 1949.
     313 pp.

     Holds the view that movements rising out of economic
distress drift into futile third-party activity. Despite many
failures, independent parties with substantial support have
often forced major parties to change their policies.

42.   Grumm, John G. "Theories of Electoral Systems." Mid-
       west Journal of Political Science 2 (November, 1958),
       357-76.

       Effectively challenges Duverger's thesis, item 33, with
election data from five countries that switched from plurality
to proportional systems. Proportional systems are seen as a
result, not a cause, of many parties.

43.   Harrington, Michael. Toward a Democratic Left: A Radical
       Program for a New Majority. New York: Macmillan, 1968.
       314 pp.

       Recommends a program of massive public investment, to
eradicate slums and provide full employment, but concludes that
the democratic left should capture the Democratic Party rather
than launch a third party.

44.   Hartz, Louis. The Liberal Tradition in America: An Inter-
       pretation of American Political Thought Since the Revo-
       lution. New York: Harcourt, Brace and World, 1955.
       329 pp.

       Advances the thesis that the lack of a feudal tradition
contributed heavily to the dominance of Lockean liberalism among
most American political parties. This interpretation is frequently cited by scholars who see social consensus producing
two strong parties with similar views.

45.   Haynes, Fred E. Social Politics in the United States.
       Boston: Houghton Mifflin, 1924. 414 pp.

       An enthusiastic, progressive scholar expresses the view
that a series of minor parties demanded government efforts to
achieve social and economic change and by 1912 had attracted a
strong majority to their side.

46.   _____. Third Party Movements Since the Civil War with
       Special Reference to Iowa: A Study in Social Politics.
       Iowa City: State Historical Society, 1916. 564 pp.

       Holds that third parties are highly significant because
they force the major parties to respond to the protests of people demanding social and economic reform. Similar themes as
item 45 with less discussion of socialism.

47.   Hermens, F.A. <u>Democracy or Anarchy? A Study of Propor-
       tional Representation</u>. New York: Johnson, 1941; reprint
       ed., 1972. 491 pp.

       Advocates the view that proportional representation
would quickly replace the American two-party system with at
least four parties. With the present majority system, third
parties are forced to rejoin the major parties.

48.   Herring, Pendleton. <u>The Politics of Democracy: American
       Parties in Action</u>. New York: W.W. Norton, 1940. 468
       pp.

       Chapter on the significance of third parties is still
a valuable summary of major issues. Third-party influence has
been limited by the flexibility of the major parties, the method
of electing the president and the specific and radical nature
of minor party proposals.

49.   Hesseltine, William B. <u>The Rise and Fall of Third Par-
       ties: From Anti-Masonry to Wallace</u>. Gloucester, Mass.:
       Peter Smith, 1948. Reprint ed., 1957. 119 pp.

       Blames the progressives' failure to unite on their ten-
dency to work within the conservative major parties and on the
difficulty of satisfying both farmers and laborers. Partisan
author believes a liberal party is needed to save the nation.

50.   _____. <u>Third-Party Movements in the United States</u>.
       Princeton, N.J.: D. Van Nostrand, 1962. 191 pp.

       Describes all third parties from Anti-Masons to the
Dixiecrats and concludes that their chief role is forcing the
major parties to adjust their programs to achieve greater
national unity. Contains twenty-six selected documents of
interest.

51.   Hicks, John D. "The Third Party Tradition in American
       Politics." <u>Mississippi Valley Historical Review</u> 20
       (June, 1933): 3-28.

       Claims that third parties had affected the outcome of
six presidential elections by 1933 and were chiefly responsible
for many reforms.

52.   Higham, John. Strangers in the Land: Patterns of Ameri-
          can Nativism, 1860-1925. Brunswick, N.J.: Rutgers Uni-
          versity Press, 1955. 431 pp.

       Acquits Populist and Progressive movements of the charge
of nativism. James B. Weaver rejected the Populists' restrictive immigration plank, and the Progressives were indifferent
on the issue.

53.   Hinderaker, Ivan. Party Politics. New York: Henry Holt,
          1956. 694 pp.

       Chapter on minor party weighs the pros and cons of work-
ing within major parties or starting a new one. Following a
helpful critique of Douglas, item 31, author concludes that
working within a major party is more effective.

54.   Hofstadter, Richard. The Age of Reform: From Bryan to
          F.D.R. New York: Alfred A. Knopf, 1955. 330 pp.

       Attempts to balance excessively favorable treatment of
Populists and Progressives with evidence of Populist support
for conspiracy theories, anti-Semitism, anti-British bias, and
negative attitudes toward immigrants by both movements.

55.   _____. The American Political Tradition and the Men
          Who Made It. New York: Alfred A. Knopf, 1948. 381 pp.

       Introduction to study of major political thinkers
stresses unity of Americans behind beliefs in the rights of
property, economic individualism, competition, and nationalism.

56.   _____. The Paranoid Style in American Politics and
          Other Essays. New York: Alfred A. Knopf, 1966. 314
          pp.

       Draws analogy between the conspiracy theories of the
Anti-Masons, Populists--especially "Coin" Harvey--and Joe
McCarthy in the 1950's.

57.   Holcombe, Arthur N. The Political Parties of To-Day: A
          Study in Republican and Democratic Policies. New York:
          Harper and Brothers, 1924. 427 pp.

       Still useful study which sees third parties renewing
idealism in American politics, but finds their number limited
by the constitutional exclusion of some issue (e.g., religion)
and the method of presidential election.

58.   Hyman, Sidney. <u>The Politics of Consensus</u>. New York:
       Random House, 1968. 274 pp.

       Develops the view that American society's divisive ten-
dencies are usually controlled by the consensus-producing influence of constitutional structure, national parties, and wise
leaders.

59.   Key, V.O., Jr. <u>Politics, Parties, and Pressure Groups</u>.
       5th ed. New York: Thomas Y. Crowell, 1964. 738 pp.

       Draws helpful distinction between economic protest and
secessionist parties which exert significant influence on the
major parties and continuing, doctrinal parties which do not.
Key questions the view that Wilson would not have won if Roosevelt had not run as a third-party candidate.

60.   Kleppner, Paul. <u>The Cross of Culture: A Social Analysis
       of Midwestern Politics, 1850-1900</u>. New York: Free
       Press, 1970. 402 pp.

       Establishes an important pietistic contribution to the
support of minor parties and the Bryan Democrats in the nineteenth century, through the use of single-state election analy-
ses.

61.   Kornhauser, William. <u>The Politics of Mass Society</u>. New
       York: Free Press, 1959. 256 pp.

       Contention that mass movements of isolated individuals
are most likely to occur in periods of rapid industrialization
and urbanization, is theoretically interesting to students of
third parties.

62.   Kramer, Dale. <u>The Wild Jackasses: The American Farmer
       in Revolt</u>. New York: Hastings House, 1956. 260 pp.

       An admiring paean for the heroes of the farmers' move-
ment from Donnelly to Reno, which contends that farmers achieved
their goals wholly or in modified form.

63.   Ladd, Everett C., Jr. <u>American Political Parties: Social
       Change and Political Response</u>. New York: W. W. Norton,
       1970. 323 pp.

       The slowness of response by the major parties to chang-
ing conditions may result in decreased party loyalty and voter
turnout, electoral uncertainty or third-party protests.

64.   _____, and Charles D. Hadley. Transformations of the
        American Party System: Political Coalitions from the
        New Deal to the 1970s. New York: W. W. Norton, 1975.
        371 pp.

        Finds that the major-party, presidential-nomination
process is increasingly influenced by ideological activists
which opens the door for moderate third parties. Anderson's
independent candidacy in 1980 appears to support this thesis.

65.   Lasch, Christopher. The Agony of the American Left.
        New York: Random House, 1966. 212 pp.

        Attributes the failure of radical political movements,
from populism in the 1890s to students in the 1960s, to confusion over goals, acceptance of piecemeal change and coalitions
with non-radical parties. Any new party of the left needs to
raise consciousness rather than seek short-run power.

66.   Lipset, Seymour M. "Party Systems and the Representation
        of Social Groups." European Journal of Sociology 1
        (Spring, 1960): 50-85.

        Claims that social divisions in the United States
resemble those in France, but do not produce a multi-party
system because of American political institutions.

67.   _____. Political Man: The Social Bases of Politics.
        Garden City, N.Y.: Doubleday, 1960. 477 pp.

        Attempts to link Populism with the Klan in the 1920s
and McCarthyism in the 1950s on the basis of limited evidence.

68.   _____. "The American Party System: Concluding Obser-
        vations." Party Coalitions in the 1980s (item 69):
        423-40.

        Again emphasizing the importance of institutions to
the two-party system, the author claims that without the
national election of a single president, major party coalitions
would splinter into eight factions or parties.

69.   _____, ed. Party Coalitions in the 1980s. San Fran-
        cisco: Institute for Contemporary Studies, 1981.
        480 pp.

        Contains items 68, 83, and 588.

70. Longley, Lawrence D., and Alan G. Braun. The Politics
     of Electoral College Reform. New Haven: Yale Univer-
     sity Press, 1972. 222 pp.

     Concedes that the election of a single president sup-
ports the two-party system, but denies that the electoral
college method does so more than the direct vote proposal.

71. McConnell, Grant. The Decline of Agrarian Democracy.
     Berkeley: University of California Press, 1959. 219
     pp.

     Attributes the decline of Populism, with its broad
democratic demands, to rising farm prices and decreasing farm
population. New farm groups pursued class demands by non-
partisan methods.

72. McCormick, Richard P. The Second American Party System:
     Party Formation in the Jacksonian Era. Chapel Hill:
     University of North Carolina Press, 1966. 389 pp.

     Advances the thesis that successive contests for the
presidency between 1824 and 1840 with popular voting for elec-
tors was the major impetus behind the development of two major
parties.

73. McKean, Dayton D. Party and Pressure Politics. Boston:
     Houghton Mifflin, 1949. 712 pp.

     Contends that third parties of the past took up issues
avoided by the major parties and influenced elections, but are
in decline because dissatisfied groups use the direct primary
and pressure groups to be heard.

74. McRae, Duncan, Jr., and James A. Meldrum. "Critical
     Elections in Illinois: 1888-1958." The American Poli-
     tical Science Review 54 (September, 1960): 669-83.

     Uses factor analysis of county-level voting data to
conclude that third-party voting, especially in 1924, was a
halfway house for voters moving from the Republicans to the
Democrats.

75. Macy, Jesse. Political Parties in the United States,
     1846-1861. New York: Macmillan, 1918. 33 pp.

     Admonishes men of intelligence and conviction to work
within the major parties because third parties may be corrupt,
focus on one issue only, and confuse the electorate.

76.   Mayer, Lawrence C., and John H. Burnett. Politics in
       Industrial Societies. New York: Wiley, 1977. 388 pp.

       Rejects conclusions of Duverger, item 33, and Hermens,
item 47, and argues that cultural factors determine the number of parties in a society.

77.   Mazmanian, Daniel A. Third Parties in Presidential
       Elections. Washington: Brookings, 1974. 163 pp.

       Proposes standard ballot access laws with minimal ob-
stacles for third parties after a comprehensive review of major
issues. Concludes that third parties are significant in rais-
ing issues.

78.   Merriam, Charles E., and Harold F. Gosnell. The Ameri-
       can Party System: An Introduction to the Study of
       Political Parties in the United States. New York:
       Macmillan, 1949. 530 pp.

       Attributes the two-party system in the United States
to cultural homogeneity, consensus on political and economic
ideas, religious tolerance, and the election of the president
by an electoral college majority. Third parties are viewed
as exerting strong impact on the policy stands of the major
parties.

79.   Nash, Howard P., Jr. Third Parties in American Politics.
       Washington: Public Affairs Press, 1959. 326 pp.

       Detailed description of past third parties fails to
reach any conclusions on their historical or political significance.

80.   Nye, Russel B. Midwestern Progressive Politics: A His-
       torical Study of Its Origins and Development, 1870-
       1958. East Lansing: Michigan State University Press,
       1959. 348 pp.

       Claims that midwestern progressives from the Grangers
to the LaFollette Progressives favored specific, sensible programs of government intervention to restore competition and
equity to the economy. By 1916, the movement had achieved
most of its goals.

81. Ogden, Daniel M., Jr., and Arthur L. Peterson. Electing the President. Rev. ed. San Francisco: Chandler, 1968. 335 pp.

Third parties are discouraged because they have no chance of winning in the separate election of a single chief executive.

82. Peirce, Neal R., and Lawrence D. Longley. The People's President: The Electoral College in American History and the Direct Vote Alternative. Rev. ed. New Haven: Yale University Press, 1981. 342 pp.

Argues that under the direct vote plan voters would still be reluctant to waste votes on third parties and regional parties would be weakened. Social consensus is the basic support of the present party system.

83. Penniman, Howard, ed. 4th ed. Sait's American Parties and Elections. New York: Appleton-Century-Crofts, 1948. 668 pp.

Warns that the policy impact of third parties may be easily overstated. Free Soilers and Populists are seen as opposites with the Populists exerting the greater influence.

84. Phillips, Howard. "More Independent Presidential Candidacies?" Party Coalitions in the 1980s (item 69): pp. 395-403.

Predicts that future elections will feature formidable independent candidates from the liberal left or the new right because of easier ballot access and more media recognition.

85. Phillips, Kevin P. Post-Conservative America: People, Politics and Ideology in a Time of Crisis. New York: Random House, 1982. 261 pp.

Former proponent of a new Republican majority in The Emerging Republican Majority (1969), predicts three or more parties based on ideological and cultural divisions within the major parties. Institutional barriers to third parties are seen as insufficient to preserve two-party control.

86.   Pinard, Maurice. The Rise of a Third Party: A Study in
       Crisis Politics. Englewood Cliffs, N.J.: Prentice-
       Hall, 1971. 285 pp.

       Advances the general thesis, based on a study of the
Social Credit Party in Canada, that third parties are most
likely to emerge in areas of one-party dominance.

87.   Pomper, Gerald M., with Susan S. Lederman. Elections in
       America: Control and Influence in Democratic Politics.
       2nd ed. New York: Longman, 1980. 256 pp.

       The indivisible presidency, not the electoral college
or single-member districts, is the major institutional support
of the two-party system. Agreement on important social questions is even more basic.

88.   Power, Max S. "Logic and Legitimacy: On Understanding
       the Electoral College Controversy." Perspectives on
       Presidential Selection. Ed. by Donald R. Matthews.
       Washington: Brookings, 1973, pp. 204-37.

       Cautious, balanced discussion of the impact of the elec-
toral college and direct vote alternative on the party system;
refuses to come down clearly on either side.

89.   Rae, Douglas W. The Political Consequences of Electoral
       Laws. Rev. ed. New Haven: Yale University Press, 1971.
       203 pp.

       Study of twenty liberal democracies over twenty years
concludes that proportional representation is neither a necessary nor sufficient condition for the development of new parties.

90.   Ranney, Austin, and Willmoore Kendall. Democracy and the
       American Party System. 1956 reprint ed. Westport,
       Conn.: Greenwood Press, 1974. 550 pp.

       Finds that third parties are most important as safety
valves for discontented groups, with interest groups holding
greater policy influence. Contains useful review of major
third parties.

91.   Rice, Stuart A. <u>Farmers and Workers in American Politics</u>.
       1924 reprint ed. New York: AMS Press, 1969. 231 pp.

       With objectivity lacking in many other studies of his
time, the author concludes that farmer-worker coalitions are
pushed together by some economic and political form issues but
pulled apart by other economic and social issues.

92.   Robinson, Edgar E. <u>The Evolution of American Political</u>
       <u>Parties: A Sketch of Party Development</u>. New York: Har-
       court, Brace, 1924. 382 pp.

       Holds that changing economic conditions in the late
nineteenth century required the formation of a new party to
improve the conditions of the average farmer and worker.

93.   Rogin, Michael P. <u>The Intellectuals and McCarthy: The</u>
       <u>Radical Specter</u>. Cambridge, Mass.: M.I.T. Press, 1967.
       366 pp.

       Challenges pluralist scholars who have linked agrarian
third parties with McCarthyism in the 1950s by showing different
bases of support for the two movements in Wisconsin and the
Dakotas.

94.   Rohlfing, Charles C., and James C. Charlesworth, ed.
       "Parties and Politics: 1948." <u>The Annals of the Ameri-</u>
       <u>can Academy of Political and Social Science</u> 259 (Sep-
       tember, 1948): 1-152.

       Contains items 27, 111, and 114.

95.   Roseboom, Eugene H. <u>A History of Presidential Elections</u>.
       New York: Macmillan, 1959. 568 pp.

       Description of elections, including those of 1892, 1912,
and 1948 with important third parties, shows that progressive
senators were split in 1912 between Roosevelt and Wilson.

96.   Rosenstone, Steven J., Roy L. Behr, and Edward H. Lazarus.
       <u>Third Parties in America: Citizen Response to Major</u>
       <u>Party Failure</u>. Princeton, N.J.: Princeton University
       Press, 1984. 266 pp.

       Attributes third-party voting to the failure of the
major parties to address important issues, the availability of
well-known candidates and a low level of loyalty to the major
parties near the end of a party system. Statistical model

developed predicts that a third party might win as much as 10 percent.

97.   Rossiter, Clinton. Parties and Politics in America.
          Ithaca, N.Y.: Cornell University Press, 1960. 205 pp.

          Creates third-party categories, suggesting that the Populists may have been the only minor party with the potential to become a major party, and adopts a conventional, multiple-cause explanation of two-partyism.

98.   Rusher, William A. The Making of the New Majority Par-
          ty. New York: Sheed and Ward, 1975. 22 pp.

          Attributes the two-party system to the independent election of the president, the homogenization of society, and major party co-optation of third parties. He recommends that economic and social conservatives join in a new party to replace the Republicans. No footnotes or index.

99.   Saloutos, Theodore. Farmer Movements in the South, 1865-
          1933. Berkeley: University of California Press, 1960.
          354 pp.

          Claims that Southern farmers, before and after their split on the third-party issue in 1892, worked within the Democratic Party and contributed significant ideas to Wilsonian and New Deal farm legislation.

100.   Sayre, Wallace S., and Judith H. Parris. Voting for
          President: The Electoral College and the American
          Political System. Washington: Brookings, 1970. 169
          pp.

          Contends that the direct vote plan would encourage minor parties, while the electoral college minimizes their strength by encouraging political leaders to work within two major parties.

101.   Schattschneider, E.E. Party Government. New York: Holt,
          Rinehart and Winston, 1942. 219 pp.

          The American two-party system is seen as a direct consequence of single-member district elections. Sectional parties are prevented by the presidential election.

102.   Shannon, Fred A. American Farmers' Movements. Prince-
       ton, N.J.: D. Van Nostrand, 1957. 192 pp.

       Description of farmers' political organizations claims
that the strongest one, the Populists, should be credited with
prophetic insight rather than immediate legislative success.

103.   Shively, W. Phillips. "The Elusive 'Psychological Fac-
       tor': A Test for the Impact of Electoral Systems on
       Voters' Behavior." Comparative Politics 3 (October,
       1970): 115-25.

       Rejects the belief that voters turn away from third
parties to avoid wasting their votes through correlation of
district election results in Britain and Germany.

104.   Sindler, Allan P. Political Parties in the United
       States. New York: St. Martin's Press, 1966. 117 pp.

       Concludes that social consensus is more important than
institutional factors in discouraging minor parties. Also predicts that a third party based on racial issues may develop but
will not survive.

105.   Smallwood, Frank. The Other Candidates: Third Parties
       in Presidential Elections. Hanover, N.H.: University
       Press of New England, 1983. 317 pp.

       Conventional discussion of the causes of the two-
party system and the role of third parties is supplemented by
specific proposals for changing ballot access laws, the campaign finance act and televised debates to increase fairness
for all parties.

106.   Sorauf, Frank J. Party Politics in America. 4th ed.
       Boston: Little, Brown, 1980. 436 pp.

       Divides causes of two-partyism into institutional,
dualist, cultural, and consensual theories without clearly
differentiating among the non-institutional causes. With
easier ballot and media access, third party and independent
candidates may run more often.

107.   _____. Political Parties in the American System.
       Boston: Little, Brown, 1964. 194 pp.

       Attributes the decline of third parties to the dwin-
dling number of small, family farmers in the plains and prairie

states and the disappearance of regions with distinctive features.

108.   Stedman, Murray S., and Susan W. Stedman. <u>Discontent</u>
            <u>at the Polls: A Study of Farmer and Labor Parties,</u>
            <u>1827-1948.</u> 1950 reprint. New York: Russell and Rus-
            sell, 1967. 190 pp.

        The major role of farmer-labor parties has been to
express discontent and popularize ideas. The limited success
of these mostly moderate parties is attributed to wariness of
class parties, loyalty to existing parties, apathy, and lack
of awareness.

109.   Sundquist, James L. <u>Dynamics of the Party System: Align-</u>
            <u>ment and Realignment of Political Parties in the United</u>
            <u>States.</u> Washington: Brookings, 1973. 388 pp.

        Describes third parties from the Liberty party to the
American Independents to illustrate his general theory. Third
parties form when the major parties leave one polar force unrep-
resented on a new, polarizing issue.

110.   Taylor, Carl C. <u>The Farmers' Movement, 1620-1920.</u> New
            York: American Book, 1953. 519 pp.

        Claims that farmers' continuing political activity
was an effort to protect their economic interests in a commer-
cial, capitalist system. After the Populists, farmers chose
lobbying tactics over third-party formation.

111.   Thomas, Norman. "Do Left-Wing Parties Belong in Our
            System?" <u>The Annals of the American Academy of Poli-</u>
            <u>tical and Social Science</u> (item 94): 24-29.

        Claims significant policy impact for third parties,
but blames the electoral college and ballot access problems
for the lack of greater electoral success.

112.   Turner, Frederick J. <u>The Frontier in American History.</u>
            New York: Henry Holt, 1920. 375 pp.

        Contains Turner's original 1893 essay on the frontier'
impact on American culture and politics along with later essays
including his "Contributions of the West to American Democracy"
from 1903.

113.   The Twentieth Century Fund. _Winner Take All: Report_
        of the Twentieth Century Fund Task Force on Reform
        of the Presidential Election Process. New York:
        Holmes and Meier, 1978. 82 pp.

            Contends that the national bonus plan for electing
        the president would neither encourage regional third parties
        as does the present system, nor attract more candidates as the
        direct election plan with runoff might do. Well-written back-
        ground paper by William R. Keech is included.

114.   Wallace, Henry A. "Why a Third Party in 1948?" _The_
        Annals of the American Academy of Political and Social
        Science (item 94): 10-16.

            Acknowledges that third parties are usually transitory
        despite their impact on policy, but predicts that his new,
        progressive party will be a continuing, major party.

115.   Walton, Hanes, Jr. _The Negro in Third Party Politics._
        Philadelphia: Dorrance, 1969. 123 pp.

            Finds, unsurprisingly, that the strongest Negro par-
        ticipation occurred in those third parties which were most
        supportive of Negro goals of equality and justice.

116.   Wayne, Stephen J. _The Road to the White House: The_
        Politics of Presidential Elections. New York: St.
        Martin's Press, 1980. 269 pp.

            Review of presidential election reform proposals con-
        cludes that only the national bonus plan would discourage
        minor parties more than the present electoral college system.

117.   Wilmerding, Lucius, Jr. _The Electoral College_. New
        Brunswick, N.J.: Rutgers University Press, 1958. 224
        pp.

            Argues that the district plan for electing the presi-
        dent would give minor parties less chance of swinging an elec-
        tion than under the present system.

118.   Wiseheart, Malcolm B., Jr. "Constitutional Law: Third
        Political Parties as Second-Class Citizens." _Univer-_
        sity of Florida Law Review 21 (Spring-Summer, 1969):
        701-8.

            Commentary on _Williams v. Rhodes_ (1968) commends the
        Supreme Court for striking down Ohio's ballot access require-

ments because they prevented minor party voters from casting
an effective ballot.

119.   Woodburn, James A. Political Parties and Party Problems
           in the United States. 3rd ed. rev. enl. New York:
           Putnam, 1924. 542 pp.

        Declares that third parties play a useful role of
education and protest during periods of political adjustment.
Voters should not be required to support leaders they distrust
or policies they oppose.

120.   Zeidenstein, Harvey G. Direct Election of the Presi-
           dent. Lexington, Mass.: Heath, 1973. 118 pp.

        Through treatment of the theoretical issues raised
by the direct vote plan refers to Austrian and French experience to demonstrate that direct election does not strengthen
extreme candidates or minor parties.

121.   Zeller, Belle, and Hugh A. Bone. "The Repeal of P.R.
           in New York City--Ten Years in Retrospect." The
           American Political Science Review 42 (December, 1948):
           1127-48.

        Admits that the short-lived use of proportional repre-
sentation opened the door for voting along racial or religious
lines and also more parties, but contends that balanced tickets
and higher-calibre candidates were nominated.

CHAPTER 2

THE POPULIST (PEOPLE'S) PARTY

Populism was not an isolated aberration on the American
political scene, but rather the culmination of an agrarian crusade that began with the rise of the Grange in 1873 and eventually brought forth the Farmers' Alliances and the Greenback
Party before placing its hope in the People's Party. Officially
founded in 1891, the Populist Party was especially strong in
the South and West, gaining control of a few state governments
and holding the balance of power in many other states. While
the Populists were less successful on the national scene, their
presidential candidate in 1892 (James B. Weaver) received over
one million votes (about 9 percent of the total vote) and
twenty-two electoral votes. In the election of 1894, the
Populists actually increased their vote, but in 1896 the party
joined with the Democrats in support of the presidential candidacy of William Jennings Bryan and ceased to be a major factor in American politics.

Although Populism has come to be identified with the free
silver issue, the Populists were also concerned with many other
issues that indicated their desire for political and social

reform.   Many of the Populist demands, including the initiative and referendum, the direct election of senators, the dissolution of industrial monopolies, and increased government control over the means of transportation and communication, would eventually become public policy.   Within a few years after Populism's demise, moreover, many middle-class, urban Americans who had scorned the Populists as "hayseeds" would be advocating many of the same reforms that had seemed so radical in the 1890's.

SOURCE MATERIAL

122.   Allen, Emory A. Labor and Capital. Chicago: Caxton,
       1891. 536 pp.

       A Populist treatise on the problems of American soci-
ety and their solutions. A very well-constructed argument for
the evolution of society makes this one of the most important
Populist works.

123.   _____. The Life and Public Services of James Baird
       Weaver. N.P.: Peoples Party Publishing, 1892. 546
       pp.

       A traditional campaign biography (Weaver was the Popu-
list presidential candidate in 1892) which outlines the Populist positions.

124.   Bellamy, Edward. Looking Backward 2000-1887. New
       York: Modern Library, 1951. 276 pp.

       Bellamy supported Populism, and this famous novel,
which appeared before the creation of the party, was very
influential in formulating Populist positions.

125.   Clark, Gordon. Shylock: As Banker, Bondholder, Corrup-
       tionist, Conspirator. Washington, D.C.: privately
       printed, 1894. 134 pp.

       This virulent attack on the Jews is a classic example
of the anti-Semitism that undoubtedly existed among some
Populists. Clark maintained that the Jews were conspiring to
destroy American political institutions in order to enhance
their business profits.

126.   Coxey, Jacob S. Keep Off the Grass: Coxey, His Own
       Story of the Commonweal. Masillion, Ohio: privately
       printed, 1914. 76 pp.

       This is Coxey's account of his tragi-comic march on
Washington with an "army" of the unemployed. In light of later
developments, Coxey's ideas on public employment seem much more
reasonable now than they did to his contemporary critics.

127.   Diggs, Annie L. The Story of Jerry Simpson. Wichita:
       Jane Simpson, 1908. 274 pp.

       Diggs herself was involved in the Populist movement,
and this biography praises the contributions made by her com-

patriot, "Sockless" Jerry Simpson, the Populist Congressman
from Kansas.

128.   Donnelly, Ignatius. The American People's Money. Chi-
        cago: Laird and Lee, 1896. 186 pp.

        A political tract in which Donnelly emphasizes the
benefits which society would obtain from cheaper money.

129.   _____. Caesar's Column. Cambridge, Mass.: Belknap
        Press, 1960. 313 pp.

        Donnelly's best novel, this is a dystopian vision of
an American society in which dictatorship and poverty lead to
an ultimate disaster. Crudely written and anti-Semitic, this
is nevertheless a powerful work.

130.   _____. Doctor Huguet. Chicago: F.J. Schulte, 1891.
        309 pp.

        A fascinating novel which deals with a white man who
is suddenly transported into the body of a black. This work
contains some pointed social commentary and provides some
evidence to refute those who emphasize the racist nature of
Populism.

131.   _____. The Golden Bottle. New York: Johnson Reprint,
        1968. 313 pp.

        A utopian fantasy dealing with a Kansas farm boy who
discovers the secret of making gold. Not one of Donnelly's
better efforts.

132.   Emery, Sarah E.V. Imperialism in America: Its Rise and
        Progress. Lansing, Mich.: D.A. Reynolds, 1893. 126
        pp.

        Emery was a widely-read Populist propagandist, and
this book contains her analysis of the factors leading to the
"despondency and destitution" of the American people. Emery
was a confirmed believer in conspiracy politics since only a
conspiracy could have led a people "chosen ... by the Great
All Father" into such hardship.

133.   _____ . Seven Financial Conspiracies Which Have Enslaved
       the American People. Lansing, Mich.: D.A. Reynolds,
       1892. 112 pp.

       The standard Populist account of the "Crime of '73,"
this slim volume achieved wide circulation and great notoriety.

134.   Garland, Hamlin. A Member of the Third House. New
       York: D. Appleton, 1897. 239 pp.

       A weak novel from Garland's Populist period detailing
the machinations of the lobbyists who diverted the government
from following the will of the people.

135.   _____ . A Son of the Middle Border. New York: Mac-
       millan, 1923. 478 pp.

       This work contains a brief sketch of the frustration
which led many farmers into Populism.

136.   _____ . A Spoil of Office. New York: D. Appleton,
       1897. 375 pp.

       A novel which expressed the Populist concern with
political corruption and malfeasance.

137.   Harvey, William Hope. Coin on Money, Trusts, and
       Imperialism. Chicago: Coin Publishing, 1899. 184 pp.

       An attempt by Harvey to update, and cash in on, the
success of Coin's Financial School (item 138). Interesting
for its view on American foreign expansion.

138.   _____ . Coin's Financial School. Chicago: Coin
       Publishing, 1894. 149 pp.

       This book was the most successful of the many books
extolling free silver as a panacea for the nation's economic
problems. Almost all Populists had some knowledge of this
work even if they had not read it.

139.   _____ . A Tale of Two Nations. Chicago: Coin Pub-
       lishing, 1894. 302 pp.

       Harvey used this novel to develop his theme of a con-
spiracy of Jewish bankers to destroy the American economy
through financial manipulation. This work is heavily cited
by those scholars who emphasize the racist, paranoid element
in Populism.

140.   King, S.S. <u>A Few Financial Facts</u>. Kansas City, Kan.:
        S.S. King, 1895. 59 pp.

        A typical Populist financial tract in which the author
urges all Populists to ignore the differences among them and
concentrate on breaking the "Money Monopoly" which enslaved
them.

141.   Lease, Mary Elizabeth. <u>The Problem of Civilization</u>
        <u>Solved</u>. Chicago: Laird and Lee, 1895. 112 pp.

        Lease was a popular Populist speaker best known for
telling farmers "to raise less Corn and more Hell." In this
idiosyncratic book she proposed to solve America's problems
by sending surplus laborers to the tropics and by halting
immigration.

142.   Lloyd, Henry Demarest. <u>Man, the Social Creator</u>. Orig-
        inal edition Doubleday Page, New York. Reprinted
        Westport, Conn.: Hyperion Press, 1975. 279 pp.

        Although this book originally appeared in 1906, well
after the end of Populist influence, it represents an important statement of position by perhaps the most radical and
humanistic Populist thinker. Lloyd represented the urban,
socialistic wing of Populism.

143.   _____. <u>A Strike of Millionaires Against Miners</u>.
        New York: Johnson Reprint, 1970. 299 pp.

        Originally published in 1890, this was an account of
a particularly bitter miners' strike and a plea for social
justice. James B. Weaver, Populist presidential candidate in
1892, called this "the Iliad of the battle now raging between
man and corporation in America."

144.   _____. <u>Wealth Against Commonwealth</u>. New York: Harper,
        1894. 563 pp.

        An attack on industrial monopolies, particularly
Standard Oil, this book was influential far beyond the Populist
movement.

145.   Loucks, Henry L. <u>The New Monetary System</u>. N.P.:
        National Farmers' Alliance, 1893. 153 pp.

        Loucks, president of the National Farmers' Alliance,
argued that expanding the money supply until it was adequate

to meet the needs of the people would give new life to the
American economy.

146.   Norton, Seymour F. Ten Men of Money Island, or The
       Primer of Finance. Chicago: F.J. Schulte, 1891.
       146 pp.

       A fairly sophisticated financial tract in which Nor-
ton argued that the value of money was a social fiction
designed to enable society to function. Thus gold, silver,
or any other item could serve equally well for money as long
as people accepted it.

147.   Peffer, William A. The Farmer's Side. New York: D.
       Appleton, 1891. 275 pp.

       Peffer, the Populist Senator from Kansas, argued that
the farmers were the victims of a "gigantic scheme of spolia-
tion" which robbed them of the fruits of their labor. This
was an influential book by one of the nationally known Populist
politicians.

148.   Taubeneck, H.E. The Condition of the American Farmer.
       Chicago: Schulte Publishing, 1896. 185 pp.

       A standard account of the Populist positions which is
of some importance because of Taubeneck's influence as chair-
man of the Populist National Committee.

149.   Vincent, Henry. The Story of the Commonweal. Chicago:
       W.B. Conkey, 1894. 247 pp.

       The only detailed contemporary account of Coxey's
march on Washington. Written by a Populist newspaper editor.

150.   Watson, Thomas E. The Peoples Party Campaign Book.
       Washington, D.C.: National Watchman Publishing, 1892.
       386 pp.

       A very important and detailed statement of Populist
positions on economic and political issues written by one of
the party's major figures.

151.   _____. Political and Economic Handbook. Atlanta:
       Telegram Publishing, 1908. 469 pp.

       This is merely a reiteration of traditional Populist
themes which seemed somehow anachronistic by 1908.

152.   Weaver, James B. A Call to Action. Des Moines: Iowa
        Printing, 1892. 445 pp.

        Weaver was the Populist presidential candidate in
1892. This is his call for a national reform movement which
clearly states the Populist case.

GENERAL LITERATURE

153.   Argersinger, Peter H. Populism and Politics: William
        Alfred Peffer and the People's Party. Lexington:
        University Press of Kentucky, 1974. 337 pp.

        An excellent and thorough study of Senator Peffer's
political views. Much broader than a political biography,
however, this work contains a wealth of material on Populism
in both Kansas and the nation.

154.   Arnett, Alex Matthews. The Populist Movement in Georgia.
        New York: Columbia University Press, 1921. 239 pp.

        Age and a narrow focus restrict the usefulness of this
book.

155.   Clanton, O. Gene. Kansas Populism: Ideas and Men.
        Lawrence: University of Kansas Press, 1969. 330 pp.

        This is one of the better local studies on Populism,
since it emphasizes ideas rather than politics.

156.   Clinch, Thomas. Urban Populism and Free Silver in
        Nevada. Missoula: University of Montana Press, 1970.
        190 pp.

        Clinch has very little to say about the larger issues
surrounding Populism.

157.   Destler, Chester McArthur. Henry Demarest Lloyd and
        the Empire of Reform. Philadelphia: University of
        Pennsylvania Press, 1963. 657 pp.

        Examines the mentality and circumstances that led
middle-class Americans like Lloyd into the reform movement.

158.   Durden, Robert F. The Climax of Populism: The Election
       of 1896. Lexington: University of Kentucky Press,
       1965. 190 pp.

       Based heavily on the Marion Butler (president of the
National Farmers' Alliance) papers, this is the best account
of the political maneuvers and ideological impulses that led
the Populists to fuse with the Democrats in 1896.

159.   Glad, Paul W. McKinley, Bryan, and the People. New
       York: Lippincott, 1964. 222 pp.

       This well-written account of the events leading up to
the election of 1896 contains an insightful summary of the
Populist position.

160.   Goodwyn, Lawrence. Democratic Promise: The Populist
       Movement in America. New York: Oxford University
       Press, 1976. 718 pp.

       In this impressive and important work, Goodwyn empha-
sizes the agrarian roots of Populism and its intellectual debt
to the Alliance movement.

161.   Haynes, Fred E. James Baird Weaver. Iowa City: State
       Historical Society of Iowa, 1919. 494 pp.

       Although very dated, this book is important as the
only detailed study of Weaver.

162.   Hicks, John D. The Populist Revolt. Lincoln: Univer-
       sity of Nebraska Press, 1961. 473 pp.

       Originally published in 1931, this is the classic
starting point for any study of Populism. Hicks was sympathetic to Populism, and considered the movement both intelli-
gent and constructive. Despite its age, The Populist Revolt
is still the best history of the movement extant.

163.   Jensen, Richard J. The Winning of the Midwest: Social
       and Political Conflict, 1888-1896. Chicago: Univer-
       sity of Chicago Press, 1971. 357 pp.

       Statistical study of Midwestern politics that iden-
tifies Populism as a nativistic and economic movement rather
than a social or cultural one.

164.   Larson, Robert. New Mexico Populism. Boulder: Colorado
          Associated University Press, 1974. 240 pp.

       This solid state study demonstrates the pivotal role
that local issues played in the development of Populism.

165.   McMath, Robert C. Populist Vanguard. Chapel Hill:
          University of North Carolina Press, 1975. 221 pp.

       McMath presents a unique view of Populism which empha-
sizes its religious and social roots.

166.   McMurray, Donald L. Coxey's Army. Seattle: Univer-
          sity of Washington Press, 1968. 331 pp.

       The only book on the subject not written by a Popu-
list.

167.   Martin, Roscoe C. The People's Party in Texas. Austin:
          University of Texas, 1933. 280 pp.

       This is a solid, if dated, study of Populism in Texas.

168.   Noblin, Stuart. Leonidas La Fayette Polk: Agrarian
          Crusader. Chapel Hill: University of North Carolina
          Press, 1949. 325 pp.

       Although Polk died before the Populist movement
attained maturity, his ideas were very important in its development. This is an outstanding biography.

169.   Nugent, Walter T.K. The Money Question During Re-
          construction. New York: W.W. Norton, 1967. 127 pp.

       A very readable account of the monetary developments
that laid the foundation for the Populist obsession with
silver.

170.   _____. The Tolerant Populists. Chicago: University
          of Chicago Press, 1963. 256 pp.

       Nugent argues that the Populists had an "agrarian
world view" which led them to champion individualism. While
they were not radical, Nugent maintains, neither were the
Populists reactionaries. They were simply men trying to reform society by the standard of their nineteenth-century
past.

171.   Palmer, Bruce. <u>Man Over Money: The Southern Populist
       Critique of American Capitalism</u>. Chapel Hill: Univer-
       sity of North Carolina Press, 1980. 311 pp.

       This excellent study concentrates on the Southern
Populists and finds them conservative reformers who rarely
questioned the fundamental values of American capitalistic
society. Jefferson and Jackson, not Karl Marx, were the heroes
of the Southern Populists.

172.   Parsons, Stanley B. <u>The Populist Context</u>. Westport,
       Conn.: Greenwood Press, 1973. 205 pp.

       This detailed examination of Nebraska Populism posits
that the movement was primarily an attempt by the farmers to
wrest political control from the towns. While their rhetoric
was radical, Parsons contends that the Populists themselves
were often less progressive than their political opponents.

173.   Pizer, Donald. <u>Hamlin Garland's Early Work and Career</u>.
       Berkeley: University of California Press, 1960. 220
       pp.

       Pizer devotes little attention to Garland's involve-
ment with the Populist movement.

174.   Pollack, Norman. <u>The Populist Response to Industrial
       America</u>. New York: W.W. Norton, 1966. 166 pp.

       In this pivotal reinterpretation of Populism, Pollack
argues that the Populists were genuine radical reformers determined to achieve a socialistic, humanistic society. While some
of Pollack's arguments are problematic, this work has achieved
the status of a classic.

175.   Ridge, Martin. <u>Ignatius Donnelly: The Portrait of a
       Politician</u>. Chicago: University of Chicago Press,
       1962. 427 pp.

       This sympathetic biography captures both the good and
bad elements in Donnelly's thought and emphasizes his importance in developing the Populist ideology.

176.   Rochester, Anna. <u>The Populist Movement in the United
       States</u>. New York: International Publishers, 1943.
       128 pp.

       This work is of some interest since it is written from
a Marxist standpoint, but otherwise it presents nothing original.

177.   Sheldon, William DuBose. Populism in the Old Dominion.
        Virginia Farm Politics, 1885-1900. Princeton, N.J.:
        Princeton University Press, 1935. 182 pp.

        An extremely narrow focus on local issues limits the
value of this book.

178.   Tindall, George Brown. A Populist Reader. New York:
        Harper and Row, 1966. 231 pp.

        A collection of excerpts from Populist sources, inclu-
ding books, articles, and speeches. This is a useful introduction to Populist ideas.

179.   Unger, Irwin. Populism: Nostalgic or Progressive.
        Chicago: Rand McNally, 1964. 60 pp.

        A collection of interpretive essays dealing with the
ideological nature of the movement.

180.   Woodward, C. Vann. Tom Watson: Agrarian Rebel. New
        York: Oxford University Press, 1963. 518 pp.

        This is a brilliant biography of one of the most impor-
tant Populist leaders which provides a clear insight into the
particular problems that Populism faced in the South.

181.   Wright, James Edward. The Politics of Populism. New
        Haven: Yale University Press, 1974. 314 pp.

        In this study of Colorado Populism, Wright revised
the traditional interpretation that Populism in the mountain
states was merely a matter of free silver.

CHAPTER 3

PARTIES OF THE LEFT

America's political left traces its roots to three sources--the utopian communitarians, the ideas of Karl Marx, and the Bellamites. Although there have been many socialist parties in America, no group has enjoyed significant political success. Each party has been plagued by factionalism, unwillingness to compromise, and ineffective leadership that has resulted in political failure. Nevertheless, the influence of leftist parties has been felt. Much of America's social legislation has resulted from their efforts.

Socialism became a political force in America in 1876 with the formation of the Socialist Labor Party, America's oldest surviving leftist political party. Factions splitting away from parent parties have formed every leftist party which followed the S.L.P.

In 1901 former S.L.P. members led by Morris Hillquit joined Eugene Debs and Victor Berger (former members of the communitarian Social Democracy of America) to form the Socialist Party. The Socialist Party experienced the single greatest

American leftist national political success. However, factiona

disputes also haunted the S.P.

In 1912 the issue of direct versus political action and
the expulsion of Bill Haywood caused the anarchist element to
leave the party. Shortly after the United States' declaration
of war in 1917, yet another large group departed, protesting
the party's anti-war position. This group included many influential leaders such as Simons, Stokes, Upton Sinclair, and
Jack London, as well as the Christian Socialists.

The S.P. suffered a final devastating blow in 1919 when
members, inspired by the Russian Revolution, separated from
the Socialists and formed three communist parties--the Proletarian Party, the Communist Labor Party, and the Communist
Party. Two years later, under pressure from the Soviets, these
groups united to form the Communist Party of America. The
C.P.U.S.A. remains in existence today; but bouts with factionalism which resulted in the formation of splinter groups such
as the American Workers Party and the Socialist Workers Party,
the Red Scare of the fifties, and the party's strong ties with
the Soviets have dissipated its political strength.

In the late fifties the New Left emerged. This group
never achieved the degree of political organization or single-
ness of purpose of its predecessors. Its effectiveness as a
political force was negligible.

No political group offers a more fascinating history or
a more colorful constituency than the leftists. Consequently,
leftist politics have been a very popular topic among historians and political scientists. The definitive bibliography
of material on American socialism prior to 1953 is found in
Volume Two of Socialism and American Life by Egbert and Parsons
(Princeton, 1952). The bibliography which follows defers to
this work, confining itself to material published after 1952.

GENERAL SOURCES

Primary Sources

182.   Alfred, Helen, ed. Toward a Socialist America: A Sym-
        posium of Essays. New York: Peace Publications,
        1958. 223 pp.

        In this collection of essays, W.E.B. DuBois, Phillip
Foner, Paul Sweezy, Scott Nearing, and others define socialist
objectives, demonstrate their practicality, and suggest political action.

183.   Baritz, Loren, ed. The American Left: Radical Political
        Thought in the Twentieth Century. New York: Basic
        Books, 1971. 522 pp.

        This collection of essays in the American radical
tradition features statements made by active political radicals ranging from Daniel DeLeon to Tom Hayden. Focuses on
works that aren't easily accessible about topics such as class
struggle, women, the Depression, and revolutionary unionism.
Provides a handbook of important political statements by leftists.

184.   Clecak, Peter. Crooked Paths: Reflections on Socialism,
        Conservatism, and the Welfare State. New York: Harper
        and Row, 1977. 206 pp.

        A work of contemporary socialist political theory in
which Clecak presents his program of conservative democratic
socialism as a solution to the ensuing collapse of capitalism's
life force--unlimited resources.

185.   Fischer, George, ed. The Revival of American Socialism:
        Selected Papers of the Socialist Scholars Conference.
        New York: Oxford University Press, 1971. 330 pp.

        This collection of essays presented at the Socialist
Scholars Conventions between 1965 and 1970, represents modern
socialist thinking from a variety of perspectives. Includes
representatives from the Socialist Party, Communist Party, the
Trotskyites, and independent radical thinkers. Topics cover
ways of achieving socialism in America, social order in America, and major figures in neo-Marxism.

186.   Freeman, Harold. <u>Toward Socialism in America</u>. Cam-
       bridge, Mass.: Schenkman, 1982. 356 pp.

       Views problems in America such as crime, the condi-
tions of the elderly poor, pollution, poverty, and war as
inevitable results of a capitalistic society. Predicts the
decline of capitalism in America and reviews the prospects
for a socialistic alternative. A well-documented treatise
of contemporary socialist theory.

187.   Fried, Albert, ed. <u>Socialism in America: From the</u>
       <u>Shakers to the Third International, A Documentary</u>
       <u>History</u>. Garden City, N.Y.: Doubleday, 1970. 580 pp.

       This anthology surveys American socialist thought
beginning with selections by representatives of the religious
and secular utopian communities of the nineteenth century and
continuing with works of the late nineteenth-century German
immigrants, the Bellamites, and Christian Socialists. The
work ends with articles by members of the Socialist and
Communist parties.

188.   Kazin, Alfred. <u>Starting Out in the Thirties</u>. Boston:
       Little, Brown, 1965. 166 pp.

       This well-written memoir of Kazin's experiences in
the 1930's when socialism and communism enjoyed a brief revival
in America supplies fascinating coverage of the left-leaning
writers of the period.

189.   Lens, Sidney. <u>Unrepentant Radical: An American Activ-</u>
       <u>ist's Account of Five Turbulent Decades</u>. Boston:
       Beacon Press, 1980. 438 pp.

       Lens' account of his experiences with the Left in
America from the late 1920's to the 1970's. Covers his
involvement with the labor movement, his confrontation with
McCarthyism, and his experiences in the peace movement.

190.   Lerner, Michael. <u>The New Socialist Revolution: An</u>
       <u>Introduction to Its Theory and Strategy</u>. New York:
       Delacorte Press, 1973. 332 pp.

       A book of modern socialist theory which explores
the flaws of capitalism and explains why America must turn
to socialism. Outlines a program to achieve this goal and
envisions a socialist America.

191.   Lynd, Staughton, and Gar Alperovitz. Strategy and Program: Two Essays toward a New American Socialism. Boston: Beacon Press, 1973. 109 pp.

        Offers two essays of modern socialist theory that discuss the political restructuring of America in accordance with principles of democratic socialism. Lynd's essay on political strategy urges radicals to work within existing organizations using methods which proved successful for the Old and New Left. The Alperovitz essay sets forth a program for a utopian socialist society that would be distinctly American.

192.   Simon, Rita James. As We Saw the Thirties: Essays on Social and Political Movements of a Decade. Chicago: University of Illinois Press, 1967. 253 pp.

        Contains essays by Norman Thomas, Earl Browder, Max Schachtman, and others which review the solutions each party (Socialist, Communist, Trotskyite) offered to solve unemployment, poverty, and labor unrest during the thirties. The essays are transcribed lectures delivered between 1965 and 1966.

Secondary Sources

193.   Bell, Daniel. The End of Ideology: On the Exhaustion of Political Ideas in the Fifties. Glencoe, Ill.: Free Press, 1960. 416 pp.

        In this collection of essays Bell examines post-war political and social changes in America. It is a work of sociological theory that contains some interesting insights into the history of the Socialist and Communist parties.

194.   _____. Marxian Socialism in the U.S. Princeton, N.J.: Princeton University Press, 1967. 212 pp.

        This classic study of American Marxism first appeared in Egbert and Parsons' Socialism and American Life (Princeton, 1952). Bell provides a history of Marxist parties (Socialist, Socialist Labor, Communist, sectarian splinter groups). His cogent analysis of why these parties failed to achieve political success purports that these parties were too Marxist, too dogmatic, and not sufficiently reformist for the American political environment.

195.   Buhle, Mari Jo. Women and American Socialism, 1870-
        1920. Urbana, Ill.: University of Illinois Press,
        1981. 344 pp.

        This significant contribution to the history of
socialism in America focuses on the evolution of the American
socialist women's movement. Buhle follows the discussion of
the women's role in the German-dominated Socialist movement
of the 1870's-1880's with an analysis of the influence women
had on American socialist ideology. She continues with a survey of female activists in the late nineteenth-century protest
movements and examines their role in the formation of the
Socialist Party. Women's political activities as they relate
to labor, suffrage, and sexual emancipation are also discussed.
The work ends with an analysis of the decline of the women's
socialist movement during World War I.

196.   Buhle, Paul Merlyn. Marxism in the U.S. 1900-1940.
        Ann Arbor, Mich.: University Microfilms International,
        1976. 393 leaves.

        Primarily an intellectual history of American Marxism,
this dissertation focuses on the Marxist discussion of labor
radicalism, political philosophy, economics, and history.
Traces the growing realization among American Marxists that
their success would depend upon their ability to alter European
Marxist theory to accommodate American cultural realities.
Excellent bibliography.

197.   Burbank, Garin. When Farmers Voted Red: The Gospel of
        Socialism in the Oklahoma Countryside, 1910-1924.
        Westport, Conn.: Greenwood Press, 1976. 225 pp.

        Detailed description of the people and events of the
Oklahoman socialist movement.

198.   Cantor, Milton. The Divided Left: American Radicalism,
        1900-1975. Edited by Eric Foner. New York: Hill and
        Wang, 1978. 248 pp.

        In this historical survey Cantor discusses the poli-
tical failure of socialist groups from the Socialist Workers
Party through the New Left. He attributes their failure to
factionalism, American cultural traditions such as individualism and the sanctity of private property, and the absence of
class consciousness.

199.   Clecak, Peter. Radical Paradoxes: Dilemmas of the
        American Left, 1945-1970. New York: Harper and Row,
        1973. 358 pp.

        Analyzes the failure of the Left to gain political
power in America focusing on the views of C. Wright Mills,
Paul Baran, Paul Sweezy, and Herbert Marcuse. Offers a program
for a non-utopian socialist America.

200.   Diggins, John P. The American Left in the Twentieth
        Century. New York: Harcourt Brace Jovanovich, 1973.
        210 pp.

        Diggins begins by discussing the philosophical heri-
tage and intellectual history of the left in America. He concludes with a history of the American Left which he divides
into three groups--the World War I Left whose roots were in
Greenwich Village, the Old Left of the Depression era, and the
New Left of the 1960's.

201.   Egbert, Donald Drew, and Stow Parsons, eds. Socialism
        and American Life. Princeton, N.J.: Princeton Univer-
        sity Press, 1952. 2 vols.

        Volume One of this classic history of socialism in
America contains a collection of essays covering a wide range
of topics relating to the historical, political, social, and
economic study of socialism from writers with widely differing
points of view. Volume Two contains the definitive bibliography of works on socialism published prior to 1952. This
work is indispensable to the student of American socialism.

202.   Foner, Philip. American Socialism and Black Americans:
        From the Age of Jackson to World War II. Westport,
        Conn.: Greenwood, 1977. 462 pp.

        This work fills the gap in the history of American
socialism left by historians' neglect of the role played by
blacks prior to World War II. This exhaustive history documents official party positions as well as those held by party
members regarding blacks. Foner takes a critical look at the
contradiction between Socialist Party rhetoric advocating the
solidarity of all workers and the violation of these principles
where blacks were concerned. The writings and activities of
blacks in socialist politics are carefully detailed.

203.   Goldberg, Harvey, ed. <u>American Radicals: Some Problems</u>
       <u>and Personalities</u>. New York: Modern Reader Paper-
       backs, 1969. 308 pp.

       This collection of essays offers well-written concise
analysis and essential biographical information on Socialists
such as Debs, DeLeon, and Haywood and on men who played an
important role by influence or activity in the American Socialist movement--John Brown, Robert LaFollette, and John Peter
Altgeld.

204.   Green, James R. <u>Grass-roots Socialism: Radical Move-</u>
       <u>ments in the Southwest, 1895-1943</u>. Baton Rouge:
       Louisiana State University Press, 1978. 450 pp.

       This regional study considers the area from which the
Socialist Party received its greatest support prior to World
War I. Analyzes the political beliefs of the rank and file
based upon their voting records and describes regional Social-
ist leaders (among them, Kate O'Hare, Julius Wayland, Oscar
Ameringer) and their methods.

205.   Harrington, Michael. <u>Socialism</u>. New York: Saturday
       Review Press, 1972. 436 pp.

       Harrington carefully examines Marxist theory, evaluates
the anti-Marxist stance of many socialist political groups,
attacks American capitalism, and presents a utopian vision of
a truly Marxist socialism in America.

206.   Harris, David John. <u>Socialist Origins in the U.S.:</u>
       <u>American Forerunners of Marx, 1817-1832</u>. Assen,
       Norway: Van Gorcum, 1966. 146 pp.

       Describes and analyzes the ideas of several early
American socialists including Cornelius Blatchly, Daniel Ray-
mond, Langdon Byllesby, William McClure, William Heighton, and
Thomas Skidmore. Demonstrates the role each man played in
the formation of American socialist theory.

207.   Herreshoff, David. <u>Origins of American Marxism: From</u>
       <u>the Transcendentalists to DeLeon</u>. New York: Monad
       Press, 1973. (Published in 1967 under the title
       <u>American Disciples of Marx</u>.) 215 pp.

       After discussing the similarities between European
Marxism and American transcendentalism, Herreshoff focuses
upon the activities and ideas of Orestes Brownson, Joseph

Weydemeyer, Friedrich Sorge, and Daniel DeLeon, tracing their
application of Marxist theory to American social and intellectual conditions. Covers the influence of these thinkers upon
the Socialist and Communist parties. Herreshoff attempts too
much in this work. It suffers from lack of focus and dis-
organization.

208.   Hook, Sidney. Marx and the Marxists: The Ambiguous
          Legacy. Princeton, N.J.: Van Nostrand, 1955. 254
          pp.

       This excellent introduction to Marxist philosophy
surveys the theory and practical policies set forth by Marxist
thinkers such as Kautsky, Luxemborg, Lenin, Stalin, Trotsky,
and Marx himself. The latter portion of the work contains
selected writings by these representative Marxist theoreticians.

209.   Johnpoll, Bernard K., and Lillian Johnpoll. The Impos-
          sible Dream: The Rise and Decline of the American
          Left. Westport, Conn.: Greenwood, 1981. 373 pp.

       This significant contribution to early American Social-
ist history covers the period between 1829 and 1912. The
authors view Marx's influence on American radical tradition as
minor and identify the uniquely American aspects of our radical heritage.

210.   Johnson, Oakley C. Marxism in United States History
          before the Russian Revolution, 1876-1917. New York:
          Humanities Press, 1974. 196 pp.

       Evaluates the impact of Marxism on American politics,
labor unions, art and literature, women's activities and personalities of the Workingmen's Party, the Socialist Labor
Party, and the trade unions that had Socialist leadership. The
treatment is neither thorough or scholarly.

211.   Kraditor, Aileen S. The Radical Persuasion, 1890-
          1917: Aspects of the Intellectual History and the
          Historiography of Three American Radical Organiza-
          tions. Baton Rouge: Louisiana State University
          Press, 1981. 381 pp.

       Examines the attitudes and political theories of
members of the Socialist Labor Party, the Socialist Party, and
the Industrial Workers of the World from the viewpoint that
these groups were mistaken in their assumptions that the
majority of the workers were dissatisfied anticapitalists and

that capitalism was declining. Failure of these groups is
attributed to their misconceptions about American society.

212.   Lader, Lawrence. Power on the Left: American Radical
        Movements Since 1946. New York: Norton, 1979. 410
        pp.

        Sympathetic survey of the left covers the Communist
Party, the Progressive Henry Wallace campaign of 1948, the
hysteria of the McCarthy era, the civil rights and women's
liberation movements, and the New Left (which he defines as
any group seeking decisive change for the oppressed). It
provides a valuable survey despite its Marxist viewpoint.

213.   Laslett, John. Labor and the Left: A Study of Social-
        ist and Radical Influences in the American Labor
        Movement, 1881-1924. New York: Basic Books, 1970.
        326 pp.

        Differs with the commonly held theory that the
Socialists' failure to control American labor resulted from
socialist ideology and the efforts of anti-socialist labor
leaders. Rather, Laslett contends, their failure is attri-
butable to the unique characteristics of American social and
industrial development. This thesis is supported by evidence
derived from examining six labor organizations between 1881-
1930. Excellent, clearly written analysis of the relationship
between the Socialist Party and American labor.

214.   _____, and Seymour M. Lipset, eds. Failure of a
        Dream? Essays in the History of American Socialism.
        Garden City, N.Y.: Anchor Press, 1974. 754 pp.

        A collection of essays which discuss socialism's
failure to gain political success in America. Each essay is
followed by critical comment and a reply from the essay's
author thereby providing thorough treatment of each point of
view. The essayists include noted historians and political
scientists and leading socialists. An excellent survey of
a frequently discussed problem.

215.   Lens, Sidney. Radicalism in America. Cambridge, Mass.:
        Schenkman, 1981. 407 pp. (Originally published by
        Crowell, 1966.)

        Lens surveys American radicalism from colonial times
to the 1960's.

216.   Levin, Nora. While Messiah Tarried: Jewish Socialist
        Movements, 1871-1917. London: Routledge and Kegan
        Paul, 1978. 554 pp.

        Covers Jewish socialist movements in Russia, the
United States, and Palestine. Valuable source of information
on the European background of the American socialist movement.
Details the role of Jews in the Socialist Labor Party and the
Socialist Party. Good coverage of the Jewish socialist press
in America.

217.   Liebman, Arthur. Jews and the Left. New York: Wiley,
        1979. 676 pp.

        A thorough, scholarly examination of Jewish partici-
pation in American radical politics from 1880 to the 1970's.
Liebman's analysis of the interplay between ethnicity, class,
and politics explores the question of why Jews, who represent
a minority in America, played a disproportionately large role
in American radical history.

218.   Murray, Robert K. Red Scare: A Study in National Hys-
        teria, 1919-1920. Minneapolis, Minn.: University of
        Minnesota Press, 1955. 337 pp.

        This well-written, scholarly study provides thorough
treatment of the post-war fear of radicalism that adversely
affected the lives of American Socialists and Communists.
Murray discusses the sources of the phenomenon, the events it
triggered, and the effects it had on American life.

219.   Peterson, H.C., and Gilbert C. Fite. Opponents of War,
        1917-1918. Seattle: University of Washington Press,
        1971. 399 pp. (Originally published by University
        of Wisconsin Press, 1957.)

        Examines the people and organizations who opposed
World War I, focusing on the Socialist Party, the Anarchists,
and the I.W.W. Covers the pacifists' reasons for opposing the
war and the effects of this stand upon their lives and their
political success.

220.   Preston, William. Aliens and Dissenters: Federal Sup-
        pression of Radicals, 1903-1933. Cambridge, Mass.:
        Harvard University Press, 1963. 352 pp.

        This history of the federal government's treatment of
radicals and immigrants offers a well-documented account of

the origins and consequences of the government's discriminatory practices. Thorough treatment of the World War I red trials.

221. Quint, Howard. The Forging of American Socialism: Origins of the Modern Movement. Indianapolis: Bobbs-Merrill, 1964. 409 pp. (Originally published by University of South Carolina Press, 1953.)

A classic source of information on socialism in America from 1870 to 1901. It differentiates between the European and distinctly American elements of the movement and focuses upon the personalities that made socialism a political force in America.

222. Rossiter, Clinton. Marxism: The View from America. New York: Harcourt, Brace, 1960. 338 pp.

Rossiter directs this explanation of Marxist theory toward a general audience. Focuses on Marx's view of man, class struggle, social institutions, and the state. Provides a readable introduction to Marxism.

223. Scheiber, Harvey. The Wilson Administration and Civil Liberties, 1917-1921. Ithaca, N.Y.: Cornell University Press, 1960. 63 pp.

Scheiber's analysis of the federal legislation (the Espionage and Sedition acts) and the activities of federal officials which contributed to America's anti-foreign, anti-radical hysteria provides essential historical background and insight into the repression of Socialists during and after World War I.

224. Schlesinger, Arthur M. The Politics of Upheaval. Boston: Houghton Mifflin, 1960. 749 pp.

A history of the New Deal era which contributes to a more complete understanding of the factionalism and confusion in the Socialist Party during the thirties. Also covers Communist Party activities and government reaction through 1936.

225.   Sombert, Werner. Why Is There No Socialism in the
        United States? Translated by Patricia M. Hocking
        and C.T. Husbands. Edited by C.T. Husbands. White
        Plains, N.Y.: International Arts and Sciences Press,
        1976. 187 pp.

        This is the first full English translation of Som-
bert's classic 1906 work which views America as an exception
to the general rule that as the power of industrial capitalism
grew in a nation, so would the strength of its socialist movement. The work attributes the American phenomenon to the
American workers' favorable attitude toward capitalism and
the American system of government, the difficulty of intro-
ducing a third party into a two-party system, the materialism
of American workers, American social mobility, and the open
frontier escape route for the disillusioned.

226.   Weinstein, James. Ambiguous Legacy: The Left in Amer-
        ican Politics. New York: New Viewpoints, 1975. 179
        pp.

        Examines the history of the American socialist move-
ment from the emergence of the Socialist Party in 1901 to the
disintegration of the New Left in the late sixties. It traces
the central developments in American leftist politics, focusing upon its strengths and weaknesses. Weinstein's intent is
to provide a deeper understanding of anti-capitalist movements
so that future movements may profit from a knowledge of their
roots.

227.   _____, and David W. Eakins, eds. For a New America:
        Essays in History and Politics from Studies on the
        Left, 1959-1967. New York: Random House, 1970. 464
        pp.

        Contains articles that originally appeared in the
journal Studies on the Left. Those included here relate to
either an historical analysis of the American political economy by members of the New Left or are histories of the socialist or Afro-American movements. It reflects the ideological
development of the New Left. Includes articles by Martin
Sklar, James Weinstein, Harold Cruse, and Eugene Genovese.

228.   Williams, Henry. Black Response to the American Left:
        1917-1929. Princeton, N.J.: Princeton University
        Press, 1973. 111 pp.

        This well-organized, well-written book offers a his-
tory of the efforts of the Socialist Party, the Workers Par-

ty, and the I.W.W. to appeal to blacks. The politics of these
groups regarding blacks are described in detail. Explores
the negative reaction of black workers, editors, and intellectuals to these appeals.

Bibliographies

229.   Buhle, Mari Jo. Women and the American Left: A Guide
        to Sources. Boston: Hall, 1983. 290 pp.

        An annotated bibliography of primary and secondary
works including books (fiction and nonfiction poetry),
periodicals, and pamphlets on the role of women in the American Left from 1871 to 1981. An exceptional work and the only
one of its kind.

230.   Conlin, Joseph, ed. The American Radical Press, 1880-
        1960. Westport, Conn.: Greenwood Press, 1973. 2 vols.
        720 pp.

        Contains essays describing 119 radical periodicals
ranging from the Journal of United Labor (1880) to the New
Left's Liberation (1956) by scholars in the field of radical
politics or by the editor of the publication described. Excellent descriptive survey of the radical press.

231.   Goldwater, Walter. Radical Periodicals in America,
        1890-1950. New York: University Place Book Shop,
        1977. 56 pp.

        This bibliography of radical periodicals lists and
briefly describes Socialist and Communist organs and their
editors. The genealogical charts of radical parties and
periodicals provide a helpful overview. Thorough cross-
referencing of title changes and detailed indexing of editors
and organizations are included, An excellent work.

232.   Kehde, Ned, ed. and comp. The American Left 1955-
        1970: A National Union Catalog of Pamphlets Pub-
        lished in the United States and Canada. Westport,
        Conn.: Greenwood, 1976. 515 pp.

        Includes over 4000 pamphlets authored by organiza-
tions and persons representing the left (which Kehde has
defined as the Americans for Democratic Action plus anyone
left of that group). Entries include bibliographic information and subject headings carefully indexed.

SOCIALIST LABOR PARTY

Secondary Sources

233.   Reeve, Carl. The Life and Times of Daniel DeLeon.
        New York: Humanities Press, 1972. 193 pp.

        Describes DeLeon's political life as molder of the
Socialist Labor Party and his unceasing efforts to organize
labor. Reeve critically evaluates DeLeon's political theories
and his fascinating personality.

234.   Seretan, L. Glen. Daniel DeLeon, the Odyssey of an
        American Marxist. Cambridge, Mass.: Harvard Univer-
        sity Press, 1979. 302 pp.

        Seretan explores DeLeon's economic and political
theories but the author's preoccupation with the wandering
Jew motif as it relates to DeLeon acts in the way of a clear
exposition of DeLeon's theories and political career. The
bibliography of DeLeon's works is excellent.

235.   Stevenson, James A. Daniel DeLeon: The Relationship of
        the Socialist Labor Party and European Marxism, 1890-
        1914. Ann Arbor, Mich.: University Microfilms, 1977
        439 leaves.

        This dissertation traces DeLeon's political evolution
from 1890 to 1914. Emphasizes the impact of DeLeon upon the
European socialists, his work in the American union movement,
and his role in the Socialist Labor Party. Excellent bibliography.

236.   White, Charles M. The Socialist Labor Party, 1890-1903.
        Ann Arbor, Mich.: University Microfilms, 1978. 306
        leaves.

        In his 1959 dissertation White attributes the failure
of the S.L.P. to the power-hungry National Executive Countil
which demanded rigid adherence to its directions. As a history
of events the work is adequate, but its coverage of the S.L.P.'
ideology is sketchy at best.

Bibliographies

237.   Ham, F.G., ed. Records of the Socialist Labor Party of
        America: A Guide to the Microfilm Edition. Madison,
        Wisc.: State Historical Society of Wisconsin, 1970.
        28 pp.

        This guide to the Wisconsin State Historical Society's
microfilm collection of Socialist Labor Party records gives
detailed information about the contents of the records and
includes reel numbers.

238.   Johnson, Oakley C., and Carl Reeve. Writings by and
        about Daniel DeLeon: A Bibliography. New York: Ameri-
        can Institute for Marxist Studies, 1966. 26 pp.

        Lists DeLeon's works in chronological order with
annotations explaining where the material can be found.
Works about DeLeon include books, pamphlets, and articles.

SOCIALIST PARTY

Primary Sources

239.   Debs, Eugene Victor. Eugene V. Debs Speaks. Edited
        by Jean Y. Tussey. New York: Pathfinder Press, 1970.
        320 pp.

        Contains selected writings and speeches arranged
chronologically to demonstrate the development of Debs' ideas.
The material ranges from 1895 to 1926 and prefatory notes
indicate where the speeches were delivered or the publication
that carried his articles.

240.   Flynn, Elizabeth Gurley. I Speak My Own Piece. New
        York: Masses and Mainstream, 1955. 326 pp.

        Flynn recounts her experiences in the Socialist Party,
as an I.W.W. agitator, and as a Communist Party member. Its
many anecdotes about the people in the left and Flynn's insight
into the history of socialism, labor struggles, and the women's
movement in America make this a valuable contribution to the
history of the left.

241.   Johnson, Oakley C. An American Century: The Recollec-
           tions of Bertha W. Howe 1866-1966. New York: Humani-
           ties Press, 1966. 142 pp.

        Begins with a brief history of Ms. Howe's activities
in the Socialist Party (1906-1940's) and her involvement from
1948 to 1966 with the Progressive Party. Part two contains
the text of an interview between Johnson and Howe which focuses
on her recollections of Leftist political figures including
Browder, Algernon Lee, Ella Reeve Bloor, and Maud Russell. The
book ends with several articles by Ms. Howe reprinted from the
New York Call.

242.   Morgan, H. Wayne, ed. American Socialism, 1900-1960.
           Englewood Cliffs, N.J.: Prentice Hall, 1964. 146 pp.

        This collection of readings provides a helpful over-
view of Socialist Party thinking on issues such as labor,
politics, the New Deal, blacks, and the future of the party.
Includes the writings of Debs, Hillquit, Berger, Ameringer,
and Thomas as well as editorials from the Appeal to Reason and
selections from S.P. platforms.

243.   O'Hare, Kate Richards. Kate Richards O'Hare, Selected
           Writings and Speeches. Philip Foner and Sally M.
           Miller, eds. Baton Rouge, La.: Louisiana State Uni-
           versity Press, 1982. 363 pp.

        This collection of O'Hare's work is divided into the
following sections--socialist writings, anti-war writings,
letters from prison, prison essays, and past prison writings.
Provides thorough exposure to O'Hare's ideas. Includes a brief
well-written biography of her life as well.

244.   Socialist Party of America Papers, 1897-1963. Glen
           Rock, N.J.: Microfilming Corporation of America, 1975.
           142 reels.

        The microfilm edition of the original manuscripts held
at Perkins Library, Duke University. The collection includes
party position papers, financial records, pamphlets, Youth
and Young People's Socialist League papers, and state and
local files, etc.

245.   Thomas, Norman. Prerequisites for Peace. New York:
           Norton, 1959. 189 pp.

        Sets forth his program for prevention of World War III

246.   _____. Socialism Re-examined. New York: Norton,
            1963. 280 pp.

        Reflects back on his forty years in the Socialist
movement. Offers an historical sketch of those years, Thomas'
indictment of communism, and his evaluation of the advantages
of democratic socialism.

247.   _____. The Test of Freedom. New York: Norton, 1954.
            211 pp.

        Discusses freedom of speech, the press, and associa-
tion as they relate to McCarthyism, Communism, and the Smith
and McCarran acts.

248.   Warren, Frank A. An Alternative Vision: The Socialist
            Party in the 1930's. Bloomington, Ind.: Indiana
            University Press, 1974. 273 pp.

        Analyzes some of the problems which the Socialist
Party faced in the thirties and defends their program and
activities during that period. Sympathetic treatment by an
insider.

Secondary Sources

249.   Bedford, Henry F. Socialism and the Workers in Massa-
            chusetts, 1886-1912. Amherst, Mass.: University of
            Massachusetts Press, 1966. 315 pp.

        Discusses socialist politics in Massachusetts including
the Nationalist Party of the 1880's, the People's, Labor, and
Socialist Labor parties of the 1890's, and the Socialist Party
up to 1912. Carefully examines the reasons for the decline of
socialist politics in Massachusetts from 1903 to 1912 when
elsewhere in the nation the party prospered.

250.   Brommel, Bernard J. Eugene V. Debs: Spokesman for Labor
            and Socialism. Chicago: Kerr, 1978. 265 pp.

        This carefully documented work relies heavily on pri-
mary sources--Debs' speeches, published works, and letters.
Brommel's use of previously undisclosed manuscripts provides
new details and insights regarding Debs' life.

251.   Carlson, Peter. <u>Roughneck: The Life and Times of Big</u>
        <u>Bill Haywood</u>. New York: Norton, 1983. 352 pp.

        A well-written popular biography of Haywood.

252.   Conlin, Joseph R. <u>Big Bill Haywood and the Radical</u>
        <u>Union Movement</u>. Syracuse, N.Y.: Syracuse University
        Press, 1969. 244 pp.

        Covers Haywood's public career as union organizer and
Socialist Party leader. Describes in detail the events leading up to Haywood's recall from the National Executive Council
and the 1912 split in the Socialist Party.

253.   Currie, Harold W. <u>Eugene V. Debs</u>. Boston: Twayne, 1976.
        157 pp.

        Although this work is not a full-scale biography, it
provides a comprehensive review of Debs' ideas as revealed in
his writings. Excellent bibliography of Debs' works.

254.   Dick, William M. <u>Labor and Socialism in America: The</u>
        <u>Gompers Era</u>. Port Washington, N.Y.: Kennikat Press,
        1972. 211 pp.

        Covers the relationship between the Socialists and
the labor movement (A.F. of L.) from the 1880's to 1924.
Emphasizes the clash of personalities and aims but attributes
the failure of the Socialists to capture the A.F. of L. to the
American social and industrial environment.

255.   Fleischman, Harry. <u>Norman Thomas: A Biography, 1884–</u>
        <u>1968, with a New Chapter, the Final Years</u>. New York:
        Norton, 1969.

        Affectionate account of Thomas' life by a close friend
and fellow party member.

256.   Frankel, Jonathan. <u>Prophecy and Politics: Socialism,</u>
        <u>Nationalism and the Russian Jews, 1862–1917</u>. New
        York: Cambridge University Press, 1981. 686 pp.

        Although international in scope, this work provides
detailed coverage of the role Jews played in the formation of
the Socialist Party in America.

257.   Gavett, Thomas W. <u>Development of the Labor Movement in</u>
        <u>Milwaukee</u>. Madison: University of Wisconsin Press,
        1965. 256 pp.

        The Socialist Party enjoyed its single greatest suc-
cess in Milwaukee largely because of the successful alliance
of the S.P. and labor due to the efforts of Victor Berger.
Gavett's careful study examines the historical setting which
prepared a fertile field for socialism and traces the political
program of Berger and the Milwaukee socialists.

258.   Gorham, Charles. <u>Leader at Large: The Long and Fighting</u>
        <u>Life of Norman Thomas</u>. New York: Farrar, Straus, and
        Giroux, 1970. 217 pp.

        A sympathetic account of Thomas' life.

259.   Johnpoll, Bernard K. <u>Pacifist's Progress: Norman</u>
        <u>Thomas and the Decline of American Socialism</u>. Chicago:
        Quadrangle Books, 1970. 336 pp.

        Covers Thomas' political life from 1928 to 1968.
Describes his role in the disintegration of the Socialist
Party attributing its demise, in large part, to Thomas' failure
as a politician. Good coverage of the S.P. in its declining
years.

260.   Kreuter, Kent, and Gretchen Kreuter. <u>An American Dis-</u>
        <u>senter: The Life of Algie Martin Simons, 1870-1950</u>.
        Lexington: University of Kentucky Press, 1969. 236
        pp.

        This well-written biography of the controversial
Socialist Party leader Algie Simons examines his political
evolution from a member of the S.P. left wing towards reformism
to his rejection of the party over its stand on World War I.

261.   Miller, Sally M. <u>Victor Berger and the Promise of Con-</u>
        <u>structive Socialism, 1910-1920</u>. Westport, Conn.:
        Greenwood, 1973. 275 pp.

        Examines Berger's public life recounting his role in
local, state, and national politics. Discusses the reformist
influence of Berger and his followers upon the Socialist Party
and his failure to lead the party to national political success
comparable to the success enjoyed by the Milwaukee Socialist
Party.

262.   Morgan, H. Wayne. Eugene V. Debs: Socialist for Pres-
          ident. Westport, Conn.: Greenwood, 1973. 257 pp.

        Describes the role played by the Socialist Party in
national politics between 1900 and 1925, emphasizing Debs'
presidential campaigns.

263.   Morlan, Robert. Political Prairie Fire: The Non-
          Partisan League, 1915-1922. Westport, Conn.: Green-
          wood, 1955. 408 pp.

        Chronicles the history of the Non-Partisan League of
North Dakota which sought to achieve socialist goals by opera-
ting within the existing two-party system. Led by Socialist
Party member A.C. Townley, the League controlled the North
Dakota government for several years and also exercised considerable influence in Minnesota, Idaho, Montana, Wisconsin,
and Colorado. Since most of the League's leaders were also
S.P. members, this study provides insight into a successful
"socialist" movement that acknowledged the danger in the social
ist name and the futility of third parties and worked around
these problems to accomplish their larger goals.

264.   Nash, Michael. Conflict and Accommodation: Some Aspects
          of the Political Behavior of America's Coal Miners
          and Steel Workers, 1890-1920. Ann Arbor, Mich.:
          University Microfilms, 1975. 248 leaves.

        This dissertation attributes the failure of the Social
ist Party to the success of trade unionism. The voting record
of coal and steel workers between 1890 and 1920 is used to
demonstrate the practice among workers to vote socialist only
when radicalized by unfair labor practices and to return to
the two-party system when their demands were met. Nash argues
that the willingness of American capitalists to accommodate the
unions diffused Socialist Party appeal and made it an insigni-
ficant political force.

265.   O'Connor, Harvey. Revolution in Seattle. New York:
          Monthly Review Press, 1964. 300 pp.

        A history of the socialist movement in Washington from
the establishment of the first socialist colony at Puget Sound
in 1897 through the anti-radical hysteria of World War II.
Describes in detail the Seattle general strike, the rise and
decline of the Socialist Party in Washington, and the subsequent growth of the Labor and Farmer Labor parties. Appendices
include personal anecdotes from some Seattle socialists and

an account of the experiences of Louise Olivereau, a Seattle
anarchist.

266.   Pratt, Norma Fain.   Morris Hillquit: A Political His-
          tory of an American Jewish Socialist.   Westport,
          Conn.: Greenwood, 1979.   272 pp.

       A detailed, clearly written study of Hillquit's public
life which focuses on those elements in his political career
which spawned criticism within the radical movement.   Discusses
his activities as trade unionist and lawyer and examines his
ideas on socialism and war.

267.   Radosh, Ronald, ed.   Debs.   Englewood Cliffs, N.J.:
          Prentice-Hall, 1971.   181 pp.

       Divided into three parts, this work begins with a
collection of Debs' writings on topics such as unionism,
socialist tactics and politics, minority groups, war, and
the Russian Revolution.   In part two Debs' contemporaries offer
their views of Debs.   Part three contains essays by political
historians evaluating Debs' political ideas, successes and
failures, and influence on American history.   Provides an
excellent overview and historical perspective on Eugene Debs.

268.   Salvatore, Nick.   Eugene V. Debs: Citizen and Socialist.
          Urbana, Ill.: University of Illinois Press, 1982.
          437 pp.

       This work views Debs as a symbol of a national protest
against the ills of industrial capitalism whose wide appeal
resulted from his realistic appraisal of the social changes
being forced upon Americans by the industrial revolution.
Coverage includes Debs' public and private life which is considered in its historical context.   Excellent bibliography.

269.   Seidler, Murray Benjamin.   Norman Thomas: Respectable
          Rebel.   Syracuse, N.Y.: Syracuse University Press,
          1967.   394 pp.

       This work emphasizes Thomas' political career.   It
also includes a substantial history of the Socialist Party both
before and after the Thomas era.   Excellent bibliography.

270.   Shannon, David A. The Socialist Party of America: A
        History. Chicago: Quadrangle Books, 1967. 320 pp.
        (Originally published by Macmillan, 1955).

        A history of the Socialist Party which covers the
period from 1901 to 1938. Excellent treatment of the three
conventions during the summer of 1919 which split the socialists and spawned the Communist Party.

271.   Steward, Dwight. Mr. Socialism: Being an Account of
        Norman Thomas and His Labors to Keep America Safe
        from Socialism. Seacaucus, N.J.: Lyle Stuart, 1974.
        223 pp.

        Sarcastic, intensely critical portrayal of Thomas'
political career which concludes that his activities "shored
up the capitalist system in the U.S."

272.   Swanberg, W.A. Norman Thomas: The Last Idealist. New
        York: Scribners, 1976. 528 pp.

        Swanberg relied upon the Norman Thomas Papers and
interviews with Thomas' friends and family for this biography.
Emphasizes Thomas' social and political ideas.

273.   Weinstein, James. The Decline of Socialism in America,
        1912-1925. New York: Vintage Books, 1967. 367 pp.

        This excellent study of Socialist Party history offers
nontraditional insight, backed by careful documentation, into
the decline of the S.P. in America. Weinstein demonstrates
that the party grew in popularity during the war and that
although the split in 1919 diffused party membership, the
strength of the movement can be determined by examining its
parts (S.P., farmer-labor groups, C.P.). The actual disintegration of the S.P. occurred in 1925 according to Weinstein.
This is a well-written work that is a classic Socialist history.

274.   Whitfield, Stephen J. Scott Nearing: Apostle of Ameri-
        can Radicalism. New York: Columbia University Press,
        1974. 269 pp.

        Details Nearing's activities in the Socialist and
Communist parties and as a political candidate. Covers his
gradual disillusionment with organized politics, his rejection
of urban and industrial society, and his utopian philosophy.

275. Yorburg, Betty. Utopia and Reality: A Collective Por-
      trait of American Socialists. New York: Columbia
      University Press, 1969. 198 pp.

      Through a series of taped interviews conducted between
1965 and 1966 with present and former leaders of the Socialist
Party, Yorburg creates a moral and emotional profile of party
members. Explores their reasons for joining the party, their
values, and their actions.

Bibliographies

276. Murphrey, Elizabeth H., ed. Socialist Party of America
      Papers: A Guide to the Microfilm Edition, 1897-1964.
      Glen Rock, N.J.: Microfilming Corporation of America,
      1975. 267 pp.

      This guide contains brief descriptions of the con-
tents of each collected series of Socialist Party papers.
Includes a complete reel list. Indexes the important corres-
pondence of significant persons.

                    CHRISTIAN SOCIALISTS

277. Craig, Robert Hedborg. Seek Ye First the Political
      Kingdom: Christians and Socialism in the U.S., 1890-
      1940. Ann Arbor, Mich.: University Microfilms, 1975.
      199 leaves.

      This dissertation offers a critical history of poli-
tical activities of the Christian Socialists in America. Their
political fluctuations in and out of the Socialist Party are
recorded--their alignment with Debs, their rejection of the
Socialist Party during World War I, the subsequent return to
the Socialists during the Great Depression, and their final
rejection of the Socialist Party in the late 1930's.

                         ANARCHISTS

Primary Sources

278. Foner, Philip, ed. The Autobiographies of the Hay-
      market Martyrs. New York: Humanities Press, 1969.
      198 pp.

      Contains the autobiographies of the seven Haymarket
victims and the introduction written by Captain Black. Pro-

66 PARTIES OF THE LEFT

vides an important view of the conditions which drew these men
into the radical movement and of their activities.

279.   Individualist Anarchist Pamphlets. New York: Arno,
        1972. 77 pp.

        Reprints the pamphlets of three important early Ameri-
can anarchists. Included are Henry Bool's Apology for His
Jeffersonian Anarchism, Lysander Spooner's No Treason, and
Edwin C. Walker's Communism and Conscience.

Secondary Sources

280.   Ashbaugh, Carolyn. Lucy Parsons: American Revolution-
        ary. Chicago: Kerr, 1976. 288 pp.

        This detailed, fascinating biography covers Parsons'
activities in the Socialist Party, the anarchist/syndicalist
movement, and the Communist Party.

281.   DeLeon, David. The American as Anarchist: Reflections
        on Indigenous Radicalism. Baltimore: Johns Hopkins
        University Press, 1978. 242 pp.

        This study purports that anarchism is an American
cultural tradition. Reviews the history of anarchism in
America and analyzes the conditions which produced it.

282.   Drinnon, Richard. Rebel in Paradise: A Biography of
        Emma Goldman. Chicago: University of Chicago Press,
        1961. 349 pp.

        A scholarly and exhaustive treatment of Goldman's
life, this well-written work analyzes her ideas and the widely
disparate reactions they invoked from the American public.

283.   Ganguli, Birendranath N. Emma Goldman: Portrait of a
        Rebel Woman. Bombay, India: Allied Publishers, 1979.
        90 pp.

        This brief biography is an adaptation of a lecture
series which offered an overview of Goldman's ideas.

284.   Marsh, Margaret S. Anarchist Women, 1870-1920.
        Philadelphia: Temple University Press, 1981. 241 pp.

        Examines the ideologies and activities of American
anarchist women of the late nineteenth and early twentieth

centuries. Focuses on their responses to the social and
economic conditions of their time and the characteristics
which distinguish these women from other activists.

285.   Martin, James J. Men against the State: Expositers of
       Individualist Anarchism in America, 1827-1908. Colo-
       rado Springs, Colo.: Ralph Myles, 1970. 315 pp.

       Examines the ideological differences between the
communist anarchists and the individualist anarchists who
believed that a collective society was impossible without the
eventual development of totalitarianism. Offers a detailed
history of the American individualist anarchist movement,
examining the beliefs and activities of anti-statists Josiah
Warren, Lysander Spooner, Stephen Pearl Andrews, William B.
Greene, Ezra Heywood, and Benjamin R. Tucker.

286.   Reichert, William O. Partisans of Freedom: A Study in
       American Anarchism. Bowling Green, Ohio: Popular
       Press, 1976. 602 pp.

       Reichert attempts a history of anarchism from 1790
to 1972. His definition of anarchists is much too broad. The
work lacks objectivity and scholarship.

287.   Shulman, Alix. To the Barricades: The Anarchist Life
       of Emma Goldman. New York: Thomas Crowell, 1971.
       255 pp.

       A popular account of Goldman's life.

288.   Trautmann, Frederic. The Voice of Terror: A Biography
       of Johann Most. Westport, Conn.: Greenwood, 1980.
       288 pp.

       Relates the private and public history of this leader
in the American anarchist movement during the late nineteenth
century. The social and economic setting to which Most was
responding is carefully documented. A fascinating study.

289.   Woodcock, George. Anarchism: A History of Libertarian
       Ideas and Movements. New York: New American Library,
       1962. 504 pp.

       Examines the philosophy of anarchism and follows with
an international history of anarchist movements. Although the
historical treatment of American anarchism is very limited,

the theoretical analysis and European anarchist history provides important insight into the American movement.

COMMUNIST PARTY

Primary Sources

290.   Communist Party of the U.S.A. The Struggle Ahead: A
        Time for Radical Change; Main Political Resolution,
        22nd National Convention, Communist Party, U.S.A.
        Cobo Hall, Detroit, Michigan, August 23-26, 1979.
        New York: New Outlook, 1979. 56 pp.

        Contains the text of the 1979 Resolution adopted at
the C.P.U.S.A. convention. Sets forth party policy on minor-
ities, U.S. foreign policy, etc.

291.   Communist Party of the U.S.A. Toward Peace, Freedom,
        and Socialism: Main Political Resolution; 21st Nation-
        al Convention, Communist Party U.S.A., 1975. New
        York: New Outlook, 1976. 131 pp.

        Contains the text of the 1975 Resolution adopted at
the C.P.U.S.A. convention. Sets forth party policy on many
issues, among them U.S. foreign policy, trade unions, black
liberation, and women's equality. Also includes Gus Hall's,
The Crisis of U.S. Capitalism and the Fight Back, and Henry
Winston's The Communist Party, Now More than Ever.

292.   Dennis, Peggy. The Autobiography of an American Com-
        munist: A Personal View of a Political Life, 1925-
        1975. Berkeley, Calif.: Creative Arts Book Co.,
        1977. 302 pp.

        Chronicles the experiences of C.P.U.S.A. members
Peggy and Gene Dennis from 1926 when Ms. Dennis joined the
Communist Youth until 1976 when, fifteen years after her husband's death, Ms. Dennis resigned from the Communist Party.
Dennis provides an objective view of party affairs that offers
insight and perspective usually lacking in the memoirs of
former party members.

293.   Fast, Howard Melvin. The Naked God: The Writer and the
        Communist Party. New York: Praeger, 1957. 197 pp.

        After explaining why he joined the Communist Party in
1943, Fast describes his experiences as a writer in the party
and his disillusionment and resignation as a member in 1956.

294.   Foster, William Z. History of the Communist Party of
        the U.S. New York: International, 1952. 598 pp.

        Covers American socialist tradition from 1793 to 1919,
then continues with a history of the C.P.U.S.A. up to 1951.
The work is not an objective history but does offer the Communist Party viewpoint on American Socialist and Communist history.

295.   _____. History of the Three Internationals: The World
        Socialist and Communist Movements from 1848 to the
        Present. New York: International, 1955. 580 pp.

        This history of world Communism and Socialism written
from a decidedly Communist Party point of view, lacks scholarship and objectivity but does provide a detailed account of
the International Congresses' programs which determined the
activities and demeanor of the C.P.U.S.A.

296.   _____. More Pages from a Worker's Life. New York:
        American Institute for Marxist Studies, 1979. 48 pp.

        Foster's reminiscences concerning people and incidents
from his career in the C.P.U.S.A. He discusses Emma Goldman,
Mother Jones, labor spies, his political candidacy, and more.

297.   Gates, John. The Story of an American Communist. New
        York: Nelson, 1958. 221 pp.

        In this account of Communist Party history from 1931
to 1958, Gates, who resigned from the party in 1958, takes an
objective look at party activities in America from its position
of relative strength during the Depression to the period of
decay following 1945.

298.   Gornick, Vivian. The Romance of American Communism.
        New York: Basic Books, 1977. 265 pp.

        Through a series of interviews with a cross section
of Communist Party members, Gornick dispels stereotypical
images of Communists held by many Americans. What emerges is
the human side of Communism. Members reveal their reasons for
joining the party and some their reasons for leaving. This
work adds an important perspective to the study of the C.P.
U.S.A.

299.   Hall, Gus. Labor Upfront in the People's Fight against
         the Crisis. New York: International Publishers, 1979.
         111 pp.

       Text of the report delivered by Gus Hall, General
Secretary of the Communist Party, delivered August 1979. Sets
forth party programs and positions on a variety of issues--the
energy crisis, Puerto Rican liberation, senior citizens, and
the 1980 elections. Also comments on the American Communist
Party's status and position on Maoism.

300.   Highlights of a Fighting History: 60 Years of the Com-
         munist Party, U.S.A. New York: International, 1979.
         516 pp.

       This collection of articles, speeches, and reports
written between 1922 and 1979 offers a documentary history of
Communist Party involvement with the American working class.
The introduction states that the material included appears in
its original unedited form and therefore presents a true
working-class partisan viewpoint of events as they happened.
The material selected for this work does, of course, present
the party line, not an objective history. Nevertheless, it
offers a thorough C.P. history of its programs and ideology.

301.   Malkin, Maurice L. Return to My Father's House. Edited
         by Charles Wiley. New Rochelle, N.Y.: Arlington
         House, 1972. 256 pp.

       Bitter memoir of a former Communist Party member.

302.   Painter, Nell Irvin, ed. The Narrative of Hosea Hud-
         son: His Life as a Negro Communist in the South.
         Cambridge, Mass.: Harvard University Press, 1979.
         400 pp.

       This largely unedited script of Hudson's taped con-
versations with Painter is both a political autobiography and
a southern social history. It focuses on the evolution of
Hudson's political ideology and his experiences in the Communist Party of Alabama. Provides a history of the party's
treatment of blacks and the effect party membership had on
Hudson's life.

303.   Richmond, Al. A Long View from the Left. Boston:
         Houghton Mifflin, 1973. 447 pp.

       Contains Richmond's memoirs plus three essays dealing
with the problem of American radicalism. His aim is to make

the American Communist experience understandable (Richmond's own affiliation with the party began in 1928) by diffusing some of the mysteries surrounding the party and clarifying the goals of its members.

304.   Starobin, Joseph F. American Communism in Crisis, 1943-1957. Berkeley: University of California Press, 1972. 331 pp.

Starobin opens with a detailed, objective account of the 1944 Browder/Foster confrontation and maintains that quality throughout. This excellent study provides an unusually scholarly approach by a Communist Party insider whose primary goal is to examine the reasons for the party's failure.

305.   Voros, Sandor. American Commissar. Philadelphia: Clinton, 1961. 477 pp.

Voros recalls his experiences in the Communist Party during the thirties and forties. Describes C.P efforts among immigrant workers. Avoids most of the bitterness of ex-party members' memoirs.

306.   Weisbord, Vera Buch. A Radical Life. Bloomington: University of Indiana Press, 1977. 330 pp.

Covers Weisbord's involvement in America's radical political movement from 1919, when she joined the Socialist Party, to 1935 when she separated from the Communist Party. Provides helpful insight into the role women played in American radicalism in the twenties and thirties.

307.   Williamson, John. Dangerous Scot: The Life and Work of an American "Undesirable." New York: International, 1969. 221 pp.

Williamson recounts his experiences in the C.P.U.S.A. from his affiliation with the party in 1922 to his deportation from America in 1955.

308.   Wolfe, Bertram D. Life in Two Centuries: An Autobiography. New York: Stein and Day, 1981. 728 pp.

Wolfe reflects upon his experiences in the Socialist Party, as a founder of the American Communist Party, and his gradual disillusionment and break with the party.

Secondary Sources

309.   Aaron, Daniel. Writers on the Left: Episodes in Ameri-
          can Literary Communism. New York: Harcourt, Brace,
          and World, 1961. 460 pp.

        This sympathetic portrayal reviews the beliefs, mo-
tives, and lives of a cross section of writers representative
of the Communist literary movement from 1912 through the
early forties. Aaron's thorough, well-written study provides
exceptional insight into the movement and this rich period in
American cultural history.

310.   Aptheker, Herbert. Dare We Be Free? The Meaning of the
          Attempt to Outlaw the Communist Party. New York:
          New Century, 1961. 128 pp.

        Reviews the constitutionality, meaning, and effects
of the McCarran and Smith acts.

311.   Draper, Theodore. American Communism and Soviet Russia:
          The Formative Period. New York: Viking Press, 1960.
          558 pp.

        An essential source of information on the history of
the American Communist Party from 1923 to 1929, this scholarly
work draws data from interviews, published sources, and previously undisclosed Communist Party documents. Draper emphasizes the influence of Moscow upon C.P.U.S.A. policy and leadership.

312.   _____. The Roots of American Communism. New York:
          Viking, 1957. 498 pp.

        This classic study covers the early stages of the
Communist movement, 1919-1922. After a brief review of the
personalities and activities of the left wing at the turn of
the century, Draper continues with a detailed description of
the political polarization that led to the 1919 split with
the Socialist Party and the formative years of the Communist
Party.

313.   Dyson, Lowell K. Red Harvest: The Communist Party and
          American Farmers. Lincoln: University of Nebraska
          Press, 1982. 259 pp.

        Focuses upon the Communist Party's efforts among
American farmers from 1920 to 1940. Detailed and clearly

written, Dyson's study explores the party's agrarian program
and the party members responsible for implementing its some-
times contradictory directives.

314. Gelb, Barbara. So Short a Time: A Biography of John
      Reed and Louise Bryant. New York: Berkeley, 1981.
      246 pp.

      This appealing popular account of the lives of Bryant
and Reed provides enjoyable reading but lacks the documentation
and historical analysis that would make it a significant contribution to Communist Party history.

315. Glazer, Nathan. The Social Basis of American Communism.
      Westport, Conn.: Greenwood, 1974. 244 pp.

      In this important study Glazer records and analyzes
Communist Party membership from 1919 through 1950. By examining the social groups that the party focused its recruiting
efforts on over the years, Glazer increases the reader's
understanding of the C.P. Party documents, information from
Congressional hearings, and interviews with former party
members were used as source material.

316. Hook, Sidney. Heresy, Yes--Conspiracy, No. New York:
      John Day, 1953. 283 pp.

      Interesting analysis of the red scare phenomenon in
which Hook takes a position somewhere between "cultural vigi-
lantism" and complacency regarding Communism in America. Also
contains a substantial section on academic freedom as it
relates to Communism.

317. Hoover, Herbert. Masters of Deceit: The Story of
      Communism in America and How to Fight It. New York:
      Holt, 1958. 374 pp.

      Hoover explains what Communism is, outlines its aims,
and describes what can be done to combat the menace that
threatens the future of America. Interesting viewpoint but
hardly a valuable source of historical analysis.

318. Howe, Irving, and Lewis Coser. The American Communist
      Party: A Critical History, 1919-1957. Boston: Beacon
      Press, 1957. 593 pp.

      This political and social history of the Communist
Party relies exclusively on public documents. It emphasizes

the effect of the party on American life during the thirties.
One of the first attempts at a C.P. history, this work has been
surpassed in both scholarship and completeness by more recent
works.

319.   Isserman, Maurice. Which Side Were You On? The American
            Communist Party During the Second World War. Middle-
            town, Conn.: Wesleyan University Press, 1982. 305 pp.

        Concentrates on the Browder years of the C.P.U.S.A.
This well-documented scholarly work challenges many traditional
viewpoints on the characteristics of party members. Using the
Earl Browder Papers and interviews with C.P. members and ex-
members, Isserman successfully reveals the human side of the
Communist movement.

320.   Iverson, Robert W. The Communists and the Schools.
            New York: Harcourt, Brace, 1959. 423 pp.

        Covers the Communist Party's program to infiltrate
American schools and teachers' unions and the actions taken
to thwart these efforts.

321.   Jaffe, Phillip J. The Rise and Fall of American Commu-
            nism. New York: Horizon Press, 1975. 236 pp.

        Covers the history of the Communist Party from 1930
to 1946. Using data from previously unpublished documents and
letters, Jaffe concludes that the party's failure as a force
in American radical politics resulted from Moscow's failure
to adapt their program to American conditions. General Secretary Earl Browder's disagreement with the Soviets over this
issue is carefully examined.

322.   Johnson, Oakley C. The Day Is Coming: Life and Work of
            Charles Ruthenberg, 1882-1927. New York: Inter-
            national, 1957. 192 pp.

        Focuses on Ruthenberg's public life--his activities
in the Socialist Party and his experiences as a party candidate. Ruthenberg's struggle against the S.P. right wing and
his eventual move to the Communist (Workers) Party are re-
counted.

323. Kampelman, Max. The Communist Party vs. the CIO. New York: Arno, 1971. 299 pp. (Originally published by Praeger, 1957.)

Traces the efforts of the Communist Party to control the CIO from the founding of the union in 1936 until 1956 when it merged with the AFL. Carefully describes the historical and political setting during the late forties which fostered an anti-communist stance among union members and precipitated the C.P.U.S.A.'s loss of influence. A well-documented study with an excellent bibliography.

324. Keeran, Roger. The Communist Party and the Auto Workers Unions. Bloomington: Indiana University Press, 1980. 340 pp.

A clearly written, well-documented account of the role of the Communist Party in the history of the auto workers unions. Covers the period between 1919 and 1949 and offers an unusually positive yet scholarly treatment of the C.P.U.S.A.'s participation in building the automobile union in the 1930's.

325. Kempton, Murray. Part of Our Time: Some Ruins and Monuments of the Thirties. New York: Simon and Schuster, 1955. 334 pp.

A classic account of the red scare which provides a perspective that clarifies both the events and the beliefs of the Communists caught up in the hysteria.

326. Klehr, Harvey. Communist Cadre: The Social Background of the American Party Elite. Stanford, Calif.: Hoover Institution Press, 1978. 141 pp.

Using information from published and unpublished sources, FBI files, and personal interviews, Klehr creates a biographical profile of Communist Party leadership through the years. Studies the changes made in the party during the tenure of each social group (immigrants, Jews, blacks, women, etc.) and the degree to which each represented the general party membership.

327. Levenstein, Harvey A. Communism, Anti-Communism, and the CIO. Westport, Conn.: Greenwood, 1981. 364 pp.

Examines the Communist Party program to control the CIO exploring the reasons for their failure and the effects their expulsion has had on the union movement. Traces anti-

communist sentiment among union members back to the 1930's
and discusses the refusal of C.P. leaders to modify their
programs to accommodate American conditions. An objective,
in depth study.

328.   Lyons, Paul. Philadelphia Communists, 1936-1956.
            Philadelphia: Temple University Press, 1982. 244 pp.

    Using data gained from interviews with thirty-six
people who were Communist Party members between 1936 and 1956,
Lyons constructs a model of local party experience. Focusing
on the process of becoming, being, and remaining a party
member in a particular setting, he evaluates the strengths and
weaknesses of party member character, ideology, and the local
organization.

329.   Meyer, Frank S. The Moulding of Communists: The Train-
            ing of the Communist Cadre. New York: Harcourt,
            Brace, and World, 1961. 214 pp.

    Ex-Communist Frank Meyer describes the Communist Par-
ty's methods of indoctrinating the inner core party members--
the true Communists. Meyers' concept of the "communist mind"
suffers from overgeneralization.

330.   North, Joseph. William Z. Foster: An Appreciation.
            New York: International, 1955. 48 pp.

    A biographical tribute to Foster.

331.   Packer, Herbert L. Ex-Communist Witnesses: Four
            Studies in Fact Finding. Stanford, Calif.: Stanford
            University Press, 1962. 279 pp.

    Using material gathered from the testimony of Whit-
taker Chambers, Elizabeth Bentley, Louis Budenz, and John
Lautner, Packer examines the question of what we actually
know about the activities of the C.P.U.S.A. based on the data
derived from the court trials, administrative hearings, and
Congressional investigations that were held on the issue of
Communist infiltration of the U.S. This study focuses on the
weaknesses of court trials, hearings, and investigations as
fact-finding exercises. This work is an important contribution
to the history of the C.P. and the effects of the Smith and
McCarran acts.

332.   Record, Wilson. Race and Radicalism: The NAACP and the
       Communist Party in Conflict. Ithaca, N.Y.: Cornell
       University Press, 1964. 237 pp.

       Investigates the adversarial relationship between the
Communist Party and the NAACP from 1919 to 1962, emphasizing
their conflicting goals and methods. Interesting study of the
Communist Party program to win black support.

333.   Rosenstone, Robert A. Romantic Revolutionary. New
       York: Knopf, 1975. 430 pp.

       This well-written, thorough biography covers Reed's
political and private life. His intellectual development,
including his ideas about society, politics, and art, is considered within the context of the historical setting. Extensive bibliography of primary and secondary sources.

334.   Roy, Ralph Lord. Communism and the Churches. New York:
       Harcourt, Brace, 1960. 495 pp.

       This well-documented, scholarly work describes the
program of the Communist Party to gain influence through
churches, the involvement of church members with the C.P., and
the official positions taken by various churches on the Communist movement. Emphasis is upon the Protestant church.

335.   Saposs, David J. Communism in American Politics. Wash-
       ington, D.C.: Public Affairs Press, 1960. 259 pp.

       Describes the political activities of the Communist
Party from 1920 to 1956. Includes data on the party's infiltration of other political parties and its involvement in labor
unions. Saposs' objective was to "re-alert Americans to the
menace of communism." More objective and scholarly works on
Communism in America are available.

336.   Shannon, David A. The Decline of American Communism:
       A History of the Communist Party of the United States
       since 1945. New York: Harcourt, Brace, 1959. 425 pp.

       This detailed history of the C.P.U.S.A. begins with
the upheaval that resulted in Browder's dismissal and ends
with the Hungarian invasion. Thorough coverage of Kruschev's
anti-Stalin speech and its effects. Shannon holds with the
viewpoint that the American C.P. members were mere puppets of
Moscow.

337.   Zipser, Arthur. <u>Workingclass Giant: The Life of William
        Z. Foster</u>. New York: International, 1981. 219 pp.

        This detailed account traces Foster's political evo-
lution as a Socialist Party member, a syndicalist, and from
1921 on as a leader in the Communist Party. Although the
biography is written from an obviously leftist viewpoint, it
supplies a valuable insider's account of party factionalism
and development.

Bibliographies

338.   Brandt, Joseph, ed. <u>Gus Hall Bibliography: The Commu-
        nist Party, U.S.A.; Philosophy, History, Program,
        Activities</u>. New York: New Outlook, 1981. 181 pp.

        This exhaustive bibliography of Hall's works includes
television and radio presentations between 1939 and 1981,
books, articles, pamphlets, speeches, and reports.

339.   Corker, Charles, comp. <u>Bibliography on the Communist
        Problem in the United States</u>. New York: Fund for
        the Republic, 1955. 473 pp.

        This annotated bibliography contains five thousand
items (books, pamphlets, and magazine articles) relating to
the Communist movement from 1919 to 1952. Covers each of
the parties initially adopting the Communist label. Appendices include works on native American radicalism, left-wing
periodicals, and the Communist trials. Contains few works
critical of Communism.

340.   Ericson, Jack T., ed. <u>Earl Browder Papers, 1891-1975</u>:
        <u>A Guide to the Microfilm Edition</u>. Glen Rock, N.J.:
        Microfilming Corporation of America, 1976. 60 pp.

        A guide to the Arents Research Library (Syracuse
University) collection of Browder's papers. Contains the
complete reel list with a description of the contents.

341.   Seidman, Joel, comp., ed. <u>Communism in the U.S.--A
        Bibliography</u>. Ithaca, N.Y.: Cornell University
        Press, 1969. 525 pp.

        This exhaustive annotated bibliography contains over
seven thousand items (books, pamphlets, magazine articles, dis-
sertations, and theses). Although it contains a small section
on related movements (Anarchists, I.W.W., Socialists), it

deals primarily with material relating to the official Communist Party in America from 1919 to 1959. It is an expansion
and revision of the Bibliography on the Communist Problem in
the U.S. (item 339).

AMERICAN WORKERS PARTY

Primary Sources

342.   Hentoff, Nat, ed. The Essays of A.J. Muste. Indiana-
        polis: Bobbs-Merrill, 1967. 515 pp.

        Ranging from 1905 to 1966, these essays demonstrate
Muste's philosophical and political development. Lack of an
index detracts from its value, but it remains the most important source of information on Muste.

Secondary Sources

343.   Hentoff, Nat. Peace Agitator: The Story of A.J. Muste.
        New York: Macmillan, 1963. 269 pp.

        Although the focus is on Muste's activities as a paci-
fist, his work in the American Workers Party during his Trotskyite period, and his relationship with the C.P.U.S.A. are
covered.

SOCIALIST WORKERS PARTY

Primary Sources

344.   Barnes, Jack, and Steve Clark, eds. The Changing Face
        of U.S. Politics: Building a Party of Socialist
        Workers; Reports and Resolutions of the Socialist
        Workers Party. New York: Pathfinder Press, 1981.
        346 pp.

        Describes the S.W.P. program to focus their efforts
on industry and industrial unions to further their goal of
proletarian revolution.

345.   Barnes, Jack, G. Breitman, D. Morrison, B. Sheppard,
        and M. Waters. Towards an American Socialist Revo-

80 PARTIES OF THE LEFT

lution: A Strategy for the 1970's. New York: Path-
finder, 1971. 207 pp.

Socialist Workers Party members describe the radi-
calization of America during the sixties and project its
results. Also includes S.W.P. documents analyzing radicali-
zation and setting forth party strategy for the seventies.

346.   Breitman, George, ed. The Founding of the Socialist
        Workers Party: Minutes and Resolutions, 1938-1939.
        New York: Monad, 1982. 395 pp.

Contains the political resolutions and convention and
committee meeting minutes of the S.W.P. during its first year.

347.   Cannon, James P. America's Road to Socialism. New
        York: Pathfinder, 1953. 124 pp.

Presents the text of a lecture series Cannon delivered
in which he envisions America as a socialist state and discusses the Socialist Workers Party's role in the struggle to
achieve socialism.

348.   _____. The First Ten Years of American Communism:
        Report of a Participant. New York: Lyle Stuart, 1962.
        343 pp.

Contains a series of letters written to Theodore
Draper in response to his request that Cannon provide information on early party history (see item 312). The letters
offer a memoir of Cannon's experiences in the left wing of
the Socialist Party and the Communist Party from 1917 to 1928.

349.   _____. The History of American Trotskyism. New York:
        Pathfinder, 1972. 268 pp.

Contains the text of a lecture series delivered by
Cannon describing the history of American Trotskyism and the
development of the Socialist Workers Party up to its founding
convention in 1938. Helpful lecture summary in the table of
contents.

350.   _____. Revolutionary Party: Its Role in the Struggle
        for Socialism. New York: Pathfinder, 1971. 15 pp.

Cannon discusses Lenin's theory of the vanguard party
and its practical execution.

351.   _____. Socialism on Trial: The Official Court Record
            of James P. Cannon's Testimony in the Famous Minnea-
            polis "Sedition" Trial. New York: Merit, 1969. 111
            pp.

        Reprint of the text of Cannon's testimony at the 1941
federal court trial in Minneapolis at which members of the
Socialist Workers Party were convicted under the Smith Act.

352.   _____. The Struggle for Socialism in the American
            Century: Writings and Speeches; 1945-1947. New York:
            Pathfinder, 1977. 480 pp.

        The majority of items in this collection were pre-
viously unpublished or out of print. It has value both as a
history of the Socialist Workers Party in the aftermath of
World War II and as a review of S.W.P./Trotskyite ideology
regarding war and American capitalism.

Secondary Sources

353.   Myers, Constance Ashton. The Prophet's Army: Trotsky-
            ists in America, 1928-1941. Westport, Conn.: Green-
            wood, 1977. 281 pp.

        The only full-length scholarly work describing the
events and personalities of the Trotskyite movement in America. Myers does an admirable job of unraveling a complicated
history.

354.   Slaughter, C. Trotskyism Versus Revisionism: A Docu-
            mentary History. London: Now Park, 1974. 4 vols.

        An indictment of the Socialist Workers Party which
uses letters, articles, and internal bulletins to challenge
the S.W.P. claim that it represents the only orthodox Trotskyite movement. Documents the struggle within the Fourth
International, focusing on Pabloism, the split of the Fourth
in 1953, the S.W.P.'s reunification with the Pabloites, and
the International Committee against liquidationism.

THE NEW LEFT

Primary Sources

355.   Long, Priscilla, comp. The New Left: A Collection of
        Essays. Boston: P. Sargent, 1969. 475 pp.

        These essays offer an overview of New Left ideology.

Secondary Sources

356.   Bacciocco, Edward J. The New Left in America: Reform
        and Revolution, 1956-1970. Stanford, Calif.: Hoover
        Institution, 1974. 300 pp.

        Traces the history of the New Left, assessing its
social and political significance and the reasons for its
decline. An academic treatment that lacks comprehensiveness
and fails to capture the spirit of the New Left.

357.   Communism and the New Left: What They're Up to Now.
        London: Collier/Macmillan Books, 1969. 222 pp.

        Antagonistic description of leftist political groups
who were "creating a turmoil in America" during the 1960's.
Covers the ideology and activities of New Left groups including
the S.D.S., the Progressive Labor Party, Communist Party, the
Youth International Party, and the Young Socialist Alliance.

358.   Jacobs, Paul, and Saul Landau. The New Radicals: A
        Report with Documents. New York: Random House, 1966.
        333 pp.

        Reviews the origins, history, and organizations of the
1960's radical movement in America. Represented are the
Students for a Democratic Society, the Student Nonviolent
Coordinating Committee, and groups associated with the Marxists
of the thirties. Also includes essays, interviews, poems,
letters, and articles by and about members of the New Left and
its activities.

359.   Luce, Phillip A. The New Left Today: America's Trojan
        Horse. Washington, D.C.: Capitol Hill Press, 1971.
        164 pp.

        In his indictment of the New Left former Progressive
Labor Party member Phillip Luce chronicles the philosophical
degeneration of New Left organizations.

360.   Teodori, Massimo, ed. <u>New Left: A Documentary History</u>.
        Indianapolis: Bobbs-Merrill, 1969.   501 pp.

        This work begins with a description of the history
and ideology of the American New Left. Teodori doesn't offer
a scholarly history but instead a European perspective on the
American movement. The more valuable section of the work
contains comprehensive anthology of articles by and about the
New Left. The book concludes with a chronology of events
relating to the New Left organizations and its press.

CHAPTER 4

DIXIECRATS AND AMERICAN INDEPENDENTS

Since 1924, the only third parties to win electoral votes
by carrying states have been the States' Rights Democrats of
1948 with Strom Thurmond as candidate and the American Independents of 1968, who were organized around George Wallace.
Unlike other third-party movements since the Civil War, both
southern-based parties stressed conservative positions and
were especially adamant in their opposition to changes supported by the federal government in the field of civil rights
and race relations.

Thurmond's candidacy in 1948 was a protest against President Truman's support for the proposed permanent Fair Employment Practices Commission and the civil rights plank of the
Democratic Party. Leaders of the States' Rights Party were
also dissatisfied with increasing federal power in economic
policy. Hope of deadlocking the electoral college was dashed
by the party's inability to carry any of the seven southern
states where Truman was allowed to run as the official Democratic candidate. Although the party proved the divisiveness
of the race issue, its success was limited to 1.1 million popu-

lar votes (2.4 percent), almost 99 percent of them from the states of the old Confederacy, and thirty-nine electoral votes.

George Wallace, who made his national reputation by his defiant stand in the schoolhouse door in 1963, opposed national civil rights laws adopted in 1964, 1965, and 1968 and denounced federal pressure for school desegregation. He expanded his base of support by appealing to voters frustrated by urban unrest and President Johnson's conduct of the war in Viet Nam. After waging the costliest third-party campaign in history, Wallace won almost ten million votes (13.5 percent), nearly half of them outside the South, and forty-six electoral votes.

While survey data does not support Wallace's claim that he swung key states and the election to Nixon, many observers believe that his campaign and strong showing had a significant impact on the Nixon campaign, the civil rights policies of the Nixon Administration, and the Democrats who, eight years later, nominated and elected a moderate southerner.

PRIMARY SOURCE MATERIAL

*   Diamond, Robert A., ed. Guide to U.S. Elections.

          Cited above as item 2.

361.   Gallup, George H. The Gallup Poll: Public Opinion,
        1935-1971. 3 vols. New York: Random House, 1972.
        2388 pp.

          Presents pre-election poll data comparing Wallace's
popularity with that of major candidates in eight different
socioeconomic categories. Unfortunately, it reports no
Humphrey-Nixon pairing with Wallace excluded in order to
assess Wallace's impact.

*   Johnson, Donald B., comp. National Party Platforms.

          Cited above as item 3.

362.   Johnson, Lyndon B. The Vantage Point: Perspectives of
        the Presidency, 1963-1969. New York: Holt, Rinehart,
        and Winston, 1971. 636 pp.

          Describes Wallace as a shrewd politician who opposed
civil rights reform with a thinly-veiled racist call for law
and order.

363.   Nixon, Richard M. The Memoirs of Richard Nixon. New
        York: Grosset and Dunlap, 1978. 1120 pp.

          Attaches a racist label to Wallace's 1964 primary
races, but a conservative one to his 1968 campaign. Discussion
of 1968 meeting with southern Republicans mentions promises
on desegregation or Supreme Court nominees. Narrative shows
concern about a third-party Wallace race in 1972 as late as
July, 1972.

*   Presidential Elections Since 1789.

          Cited above as item 5.

*   Scammon, Richard M., comp, and ed. America Votes: A
        Handbook of Contemporary American Election Statistics.
        Vols. 8-14.

          Cited above as item 7.

364.   Thurmond, Strom. _The Faith We Have Not Kept_. San
        Diego: Viewpoint Books, 1968. 192 pp.

        Writing as a Republican senator, Thurmond expresses
views similar to those of his 1948 race. On states rights,
he contends that the federal government is limited to acting
in a few specific areas.

365.   Truman, Harry S. _Memoirs: Volume Two: Years of Trial
        and Hope, 1946-1952_. Garden City, N.Y.: Doubleday,
        1956. 594 pp.

        Asserts that he supported civil rights recommenda-
tions despite the political risks and the bolt of southern
Democrats. Account omits any assessment of political gains
made because of his stand.

366.   Wallace, George C. _Hear Me Out_. Anderson, S.C.: Droke
        House, 1968. 158 pp.

        Consists of quotations alphabetized by topic from
college speeches, campaign addresses, and press interviews
from 1962 through 1967. Statements attack federal spending,
the _Brown_ decision of 1954, national Democrats, and other
favorite targets.

367.   _____. _Stand Up for America_. Garden City, N.Y.:
        Doubleday, 1976. 179 pp.

        Autobiography covers Wallace's early life and poli-
tical career from 1919 through the 1972 election. The third-
party route was rejected in 1964 because states' rights had
become an issue, but was pursued in 1968 as a protest against
the major parties, which were charged with ignoring middle-
class interests.

SECONDARY SOURCES

368.   Aberbach, Joel D. "Alienation and Political Behavior."
        The American Political Science Review 63 (March,
        1969): 86-99.

        Discovered that political distrust of government was
the only one of four alienation measures useful in explaining
Goldwater's 1964 vote. Author suggests that a powerlessness
measure might be more important in explaining Wallace's vote
in 1968.

369.   Ader, Emile B. The Dixiecrat Movement: Its Role in
            Third-Party Politics. Washington: Public Affairs
            Press, 1955. 21 pp.

        Pictures the Dixiecrats as a sectional, single-
issue splinter party whose lack of success represented the
beginning of the end of southern reaction on the race issues.

370.   Alexander, Herbert E. Financing the 1968 Election.
            Lexington, Mass.: Heath, 1971. 355 pp.

        Presents figures showing the Wallace campaign to
have been the costliest minor party effort in American history
with an unusually high percentage of small contributions.

371.   Armstrong, Forrest H. "George C. Wallace, Insurgent on
            the Right." Ph.D. dissertation, University of
            Michigan, 1970. 273 pp.

        Contends that Wallace made serious steps toward
creating a continuing third party with his peculiar combination
of populism, economic liberalism, and social conservatism.

372.   Bain, Chester W. "South Carolina: Partisan Prelude."
            The Changing Politics of the South (item 412), pp.
            588-636.

        Explains Wallace's failure to match Thurmond's 1948
vote in the coastal plains counties to increased black regis-
tration after 1964.

373.   Barnard, William D. Dixiecrats and Democrats: Alabama
            Politics, 1942-1950. University, Ala.: University
            of Alabama Press, 1974. 200 pp.

        Describes the Dixiecrats as including both men of
strong conservative principles on issues other than race,
and men who flagrantly exploited racial prejudices.

374.   Bartley, Numan V. From Thurmond to Wallace: Political
            Tendencies in Georgia, 1948-1968. Baltimore: Johns
            Hopkins, 1970. 117 pp.

        Claims that Thurmond's candidacy attracted the hard-
core racist vote in the state. Wallace, who more than doubled
Thurmond's percentage, combined racism, a common-man style,
and a defense of rural values to build support among rural,
small-town, and lower-status urban whites.

375.   _____, and Hugh D. Graham. Southern Politics and the
        Second Reconstruction. Baltimore: Johns Hopkins,
        1975. 233 pp.

        Contends that Wallace, in Alabama races and in his
1968 presidential effort, depended heavily on the votes of
rural whites and urban working-class whites.

376.   Bass, Jack, and Walter DeVries. The Transformation of
        Southern Politics: Social Change and Political Con-
        sequence since 1945. New York: Basic Books, 1976.
        527 pp.

        Portrays Wallace as a perennial office seeker who
enjoyed campaigning more than governing. Thurmond's vote,
strongest in Black Belt counties, correlated strongly with
Goldwater's southern vote in 1964. General theme is that
social and economic modernization triggered a politics of
protest.

377.   Bell, Daniel. "The Dispossessed." The Radical Right
        (item 378), pp. 2-34.

        An "old" middle-class of farmers and small-town
businessmen and lawyers, fearing a loss of status and power
for themselves and their nation, fear conspiracy and oppose
federal programs and taxes.

378.   _____, ed. The Radical Right. Freeport, N.Y.: Books
        for Libraries, 1971. 394 pp.

        Contains items, 377, 414, and 436.

379.   Berenson, William M., Robert D. Bond, and J. Leiper
        Freeman. "The Wallace Vote and Political Change in
        Tennessee." The Journal of Politics 33 (May, 1971):
        515-20.

        Study of 95 counties and 315 metropolitan precincts
concludes that rural white voters split between Humphrey and
Wallace. Metropolitan Democratic precincts, often heavily
black, and metropolitan Republican precincts followed normal
voting patterns.

380.   Berman, William C. The Politics of Civil Rights in
       the Truman Administration. Columbus: Ohio State
       University Press, 1970. 261 pp.

       Walking a tight rope between southerners and civil
rights supporters in his party, Truman adopted a cautious
stand on civil rights until 1947-48, when a presidential
commission and southern belligerence pushed him into a strong,
pre-civil rights position. Democratic party discipline and
distrust of the Dixiecrats' economic conservatism are suggested
as causes of Thurmond's low vote.

381.   Bernd, Joseph L. "Georgia: Static and Dynamic." The
       Changing Politics of the South (item 412), pp. 294-
       365.

       Finds differences in Thurmond and Wallace votes.
Thurmond did best in counties near South Carolina, while
Wallace's larger vote is seen as a reaction against protests,
violence, crime, and desegregation.

382.   Billington, Monroe L. The Political South in the Twen-
       tieth Century. New York: Scribners, 1975. 205 pp.

       General theme is that the South has made long strides
toward the biracial, two-party political mainstream. Thurmond's candidacy is described as a reaction against civil
rights proposals and government centralization. Wallace's
issues were mostly race-related.

383.   Birdsall, Stephen S. "Preliminary Analysis of the 1968
       Wallace Vote in the Southeast." Southeastern Geo-
       grapher 9 (November, 1969): 55-66.

       Correlation of county-level returns from 1968 and
five demographic variables suggests that 50 percent of the
variation in the Wallace vote is explained by the five variables. Study demonstrates problems with analysis of aggre-
gate data. In three states Wallace's vote was positively
related to percent Negro.

384.   Black, Earl. "The Militant Segregationist Vote in the
       post-Brown South: A Comparative Analysis." Social
       Science Quarterly 54 (June, 1973): 66-84.

       Examines Key's thesis (item 417) that whites in
counties with high black populations support white supremacy

most strongly. Black concludes that counties with few blacks
are still least likely to vote for segregationist candidates.

385.   _____. Southern Governors and Civil Rights: Racial
          Segregation as a Campaign Issue in the Second Recon-
          struction. Cambridge, Mass.: Harvard University
          Press, 1976. 408 pp.

      Classifies Wallace as a militant segregationist gover-
nor with progressive economic views. Wallace's defiance of the
federal government probably speeded up civil rights legislation.

386.   _____, and Merle Black. "The Demographic Basis of
          Wallace Support in Alabama." American Politics Quar-
          terly 1 (July, 1973): 279-304.

      Wallace in 1962 ran strongly in Black Belt counties,
but after 1965 black voters in these counties became a source
of anti-Wallace votes. Wallace, however, picked up strength
in the rural counties of northern Alabama.

387.   Boughan, Karl M. "The Wallace Phenomenon: Racist Popu-
          lism and American Electoral Politics." Ph.D. disser-
          tation, Harvard University, 1971.

      Contends that Wallaceism was primarily rural and based
on economic discontent and insecurity. He reports poll data
suggesting that 73 percent of Wallace leaners would have supported Nixon if Wallace had not been running.

388.   Boyd, Richard W. "Popular Control of Public Policy: A
          Normal Vote Analysis of the 1968 Election." The
          American Political Science Review 66 (June, 1972):
          429-49.

      Voter attitudes on race, urban unrest, and Viet Nam
were all strongly correlated with voting choices in 1968.
Author finds that persons opposing civil rights and favoring
the use of force to quell urban disorders were more likely to
favor Wallace with Nixon as their second choice.

*   Burnham, Walter D. Critical Elections and the Main-
          springs of American Politics (item 23).

      Contends that Wallace exploited the racial hostility
of rural southern whites and northern blue-collar whites.

Author relies on precinct-level data from Baltimore and Delaware County, Pennsylvania, for his blue-collar study.

389.   Campbell, Bruce A. "Patterns of Change in Partisan
       Loyalties of Native Southerners." Journal of Poli-
       tics 39 (August, 1977): 730-61.

       Finding that white southerners opposed to federal
activity were moving toward the Republican Party between 1952
and 1972 supports the idea that a Wallace vote in 1968 was a
halfway step in the process.

390.   Carlson, Jody. George C. Wallace and the Politics of
       Powerlessness: The Wallace Campaigns for the Presi-
       dency, 1964-1976. New Brunswick, N.J.: Transaction
       Books, 1981. 332 pp.

       Combines description of all four of Wallace's national
campaigns with analysis of his supporters. Author contends
that Wallace voters felt powerless in the face of a federal
government demanding significant social change in civil rights,
voting, housing, and education.

391.   Chester, Lewis, Godfrey Jodgson, and Bruce Page. An
       American Melodrama: The Presidential Campaign of 1968.
       New York: Viking Press, 1969. 814 pp.

       Scathing critique of Wallace describes him as a
fascist with ties to the Klan, creator of a new-police state,
and speaker who used violent metaphors and racist code words.
Reaction to riots made him acceptable in the North.

392.   Cleghorn, Reese. Radicalism: Southern Style: A Commen-
       tary on Regional Extremism of the Right. Atlanta:
       Southern Regional Council, 1968. 31 pp.

       Argues that Wallace and right-wing southern radicalism
are the products of rapid urbanization. Rooted in southern
history, this radicalism cannot be transported outside the
Deep South and will decline as the South becomes more like the
nation.

393.   Collins, Charles W. Whither Solid South? A Study in
       Politics and Race Relations. New Orleans: Pelican,
       1947. 334 pp.

       Influential spokesman for conservative southerners
describes the proposed FEPC as an unconstitutional attack on

segregation and recommends a third party which could force
the election into the House of Representatives.

394.   Converse, Philip E., Warren E. Miller, Jerrold C. Rusk,
        and Arthur C. Wolfe. "Continuity and Change in Amer-
        ican Politics: Parties and Issues in the 1968 Elec-
        tions." The American Political Science Review 63
        (December, 1969): 1083-1105.

        Analysis of survey data contends that Wallace pos-
sessed a sharply regional and racial appeal. Article presents
strong evidence that Nixon would have been elected if Wallace
had not run.

395.   Conway, M. Margaret. "The White Backlash Re-examined:
        Wallace and the 1964 Primaries." Social Science
        Quarterly 49 (December, 1968): 710-19.

        Using aggregate rather than survey data, article sug-
gests that economic and political conservatism not connected
to civil rights may explain Wallace's vote in Wisconsin in
1964, while his strength in Indiana and Maryland represented a
white, working-class backlash against civil rights.

396.   Cook, Rhodes. "Wallace Encore Focus of Alabama Primary."
        Congressional Quarterly Weekly Report 40 (August,
        1982): 2081-2.

        Reports that Wallace muted his segregationist views
and sought to build a coalition of lower- to middle-income
whites and blacks in his 1982 race for a fourth term as governor. The same periodical, September 11, 1982, estimates that
Wallace won nearly 30 percent of the black vote in the first
primary.

397.   Crass, Philip. The Wallace Factor. New York: Mason/
        Charter, 1976. 265 pp.

        Devotes five chapters to the 1968 campaign. Author
sees Wallace's movement as a primarily southern and rural phenomenon with some appeal to northern whites living near black
neighborhoods. Campaign is said to have had a significant
influence on the major parties.

398. Crespi, Irving. "Structural Sources of the George Wallace Constituency." Social Science Quarterly 52 (June, 1971): 115-32.

Combines over nine thousand white voters in six Gallup surveys for an analysis of Wallace support. Article develops an interactive model which contends that region and party identification help identify Wallace supporters even when socioeconomic status is controlled.

399. Duncombe, Herbert S., and Boyd A. Martin. "The 1968 Election in Idaho." The Western Political Quarterly 22 (September, 1969): 490-7.

Finds that Wallace ran strongest in conservative, rural areas in the southern part of the state. Idaho gave Wallace his second highest western percentage.

400. Egerton, John. The Americanization of Dixie: The Southernization of America. New York: Harper and Row, 1974. 226 pp.

Journalist believes that the racial message was the unifying element of Wallace's appeal, although the candidate exploited other issues frustrating white middle Americans. Wallace is credited with pulling both parties to the right.

401. Eitzen, D. Stanley. "Status Inconsistency and Wallace Supporters in a Midwestern City." Social Forces 48 (June, 1970): 493-8.

On the basis of 37 interviews in Lawrence, Kansas, author concludes that a majority of Wallace supporters earned higher incomes than normal for their education and occupation.

402. Ellwood, John W. "The Growth and Development of the Wallace Organization of 1968: A Study of Third Party Formation." Ph.D. dissertation, Johns Hopkins University, 1972. 538 pp.

Wallace campaign was a counter social movement resisting pressure for racial equality. The organization was an outgrowth of the 1964 primary races and relied on Alabama Democrats.

403.   English, David. <u>Divided They Stand</u>. Englewood Cliffs,
            N.J.: Prentice-Hall, 1969. 428 pp.

        Attributes Wallace support to blue-collar frustration
with welfare, opposition to civil rights and disorder, and
rural southerners, with no effort to show relationship or
priority of the three factors. Author blames the choice of
LeMay for Wallace's October decline in the polls.

404.   Fortenberry, Charles N., and F. Glenn Abney. "Missis-
            sippi: Unreconstructed and Unredeemed." <u>The Changing
            Politics of the South</u> (item 412), pp. 472-524.

        Reports that the votes for Thurmond in 1948, Gold-
water in 1964, and Wallace in 1968 came from rural counties
with high percentages of blacks and strong racial prejudice.

405.   Frady, Marshall. <u>Wallace</u>. New York: New American
            Library, 1976. 277 pp.

        Cited in many sources, this book provides a compre-
hensive biography of Wallace's life and political career up
to 1975. Author sees Wallace as a populist whose record was
marred by his racial views. Although based on interviews,
the book lacks footnotes, index, and bibliography.

406.   Gaither, Gerald H. <u>Blacks and the Populist Revolt:
            Ballots and Bigotry in the 'New South.'</u> University:
            University of Alabama Press, 1977. 251 pp.

        In epilogue, author claims that Wallace and Carter
represent conservative and liberal outlooks which also existed
in nineteenth-century populism.

407.   Grant, Philip A., Jr. "1948 Presidential Election in
            Virginia: Augury of the Trend towards Republicanism."
            <u>Presidential Studies Quarterly</u> 8 (Summer, 1978): 319-
            28.

        Shows that Thurmond did best in the racially conser-
vative Southside, with Truman winning in Tidewater and the
Southwest and Dewey in suburban areas and the Shenandoah
Valley.

408.   Grasmick, Harold G. "Rural Culture and the Wallace
          Movement in the South." Rural Sociology 39 (Winter,
          1974): 454-70.

          Interviews with 814 whites in North Carolina are the
basis of a finding that Wallace supporters tended to be either
rural residents or recent migrants from rural areas who were
defending a distinctive set of rural values. Wallace's weak-
ness in nonsouthern rural areas is not discussed.

409.   Greene, Lee S., and Jack E. Holmes. "Tennessee: A
          Politics of Peaceful Change." The Changing Politics
          of the South (item 412), pp. 165-200.

          Finds correlations of .62 between county votes for
Populist Weaver in 1892 and Wallace in 1968 and .54 for Thurmond and Wallace.

410.   Greenshaw, Wayne. Watch Out for George Wallace. Engle-
          wood Cliffs, N.J.: Prentice Hall, 1976. 276 pp.

          Describes Wallace as a racist and demagogue made
dangerous by impressive campaign skills. The prediction that
Wallace was a serious Democratic candidate in 1976 with a
real chance at the nomination was proven erroneous as he cap-
tured only 57 delegates compared to 377 in 1972.

411.   Grupp, Fred W. "The Political Perspectives of Birch
          Society Members." The American Right Wing: Readings
          in Political Behavior (item 443), pp. 165-200.

          Southern John Birchers are found to be well-to-do,
Protestant professionals. Members favor more power for states
and Congress, less for President and Supreme Court.

412.   Harvard, William C., ed. The Changing Politics of the
          South. Baton Rouge: Louisiana State University Press,
          1972. 755 pp.

          Contains the politics of each southern state in a
separate chapter. Contains items 372, 381, 404, 409, and 449.

413.   Heard, Alexander. A Two-Party South? Chapel Hill:
          University of North Carolina Press, 1952. 334 pp.

          Argues that the Dixiecrats contained two distinctive
elements. Leaders opposed to New Deal economic changes exploited the racial fears of rural Black Belt whites who sup-

plied the bulk of Thurmond's vote. Author's prediction that
southern economic conservatives would eventually turn to the
Republicans appears to have been largely accurate.

414.   Hofstadter, Richard. "Pseudo-Conservatism Revisited:
          A Postscript--1962." The Radical Right (item 378),
          pp. 81-6.

          Identifies four sources of right-wing extremism.
Two of these--ethnic prejudice and a revolt against modernity--
seem to apply to the Wallace movement.

415.   House, Jack. Lady of Courage: The Story of Lurleen
          Burns Wallace. Montgomery, Ala.: League Press, 1969.
          164 pp.

          Presents Wallace's contention that he did not force
his wife to run in 1966 to keep his national hopes alive or
to make campaign trips in late 1967 and early 1968 when she
was ill with cancer. Her activity is said to have extended
her life.

416.   Jones, Bill. The Wallace Story. Northport, Ala.:
          American Southern, 1966. 453 pp.

          Detailed account of Wallace's career from 1958 to
1965 with extensive quotation of speeches and press accounts.
Written by Wallace's press secretary, the book reveals the
paternalistic racism of Wallace and his associates.

417.   Key, V.O., Jr. Southern Politics in State and Nation.
          New York: Knopf, 1949. 675 pp.

          Chapter on Dixiecrats notes that Thurmond distorted
Truman's civil rights aims and ran well only in areas of heavy
black population and in states where Thurmond was listed as
the Democratic candidate.

418.   Killian, Lewis M. White Southerners. New York: Random
          House, 1970. 171 pp.

          Attributes the electoral success of Goldwater, Wallace,
and Nixon in the South to the region's conservatism and its
perception of anti-southern discrimination.

419.   Kirkpatrick, Samuel A., and Melvin E. Jones. "Vote
           Direction and Issue Cleavage in 1968." Social Science
           Quarterly 5 (December, 1970): 689-705.

           Comparison of the issue positions of Humphrey, Nixon,
and Wallace supporters finds Wallace voters most distinctive
in their views on school integration and public accommodations.

420.   Lachicotte, Alberta. Rebel Senator: Strom Thurmond of
           South Carolina. New York: Devin-Adair, 1967. 255 pp.   ·

           Claims that Thurmond, by southern standards, was a
liberal governor who opposed the national Democratic Party
because he wanted change to be achieved by the states. Author
expresses doubt that Thurmond would have carried four states
without the help of the Democratic label.

421.   Lehnen, Robert G. "Stability of Presidential Choice in
           1968: The Case of Two Southern States." Social Sci-
           ence Quarterly 51 (June, 1970): 138-47.

           Analysis of three interviews with eight hundred per-
sons in Florida and North Carolina found general stability of
preference. Wallace defectors tended to move to Nixon with
Humphrey gaining among the undecided.

422.   Lemmon, Sarah M. "The Ideology of the 'Dixiecrat'
           Movement." Social Forces 30 (December, 1951): 162-71.

           Describes Dixiecrat leaders as well-educated, well-
to-do men who were defending the southern tradition of segregation and economic freedom from the growing power of the
federal government.

423.   Lieske, Joel A. "The Conditions of Racial Violence in
           American Cities: A Developmental Synthesis." The
           American Political Science Review 72 (December, 1978):
           1324-40.

           Discovers that disorder is most likely to occur where
black status is improving, but where further change is blocked
by unresponsive institutions. Without mentioning Wallace,
the theory opposes his view that more force is the solution
to racial violence.

424.   Lipset, Seymour M., and Earl Raab. The Politics of
        Unreason: Right-Wing Extremism in America, 1790-1970.
        New York: Harper and Row, 1970. 547 pp.

        Wallace tried to build a coalition of conservative
anti-statists and lower status whites who objected to integration and disorder. To do this, he emphasized anti-elitism,
criticized selected federal policies, and supported others.
Anti-statists include groups like the John Birch Society.

425.   Lubell, Samuel. The Hidden Crisis in American Politics.
        New York: Norton, 1970. 306 pp.

        Argues that many Wallace supporters outside the South
actually favored civil rights laws but wished to suppress
racial violence. In the South, a Wallace vote expressed
resentment of national policies which had been growing since
the Brown decision.

426.   McDonnell, Richard A. "The Direction of the Wallace
        Vote in 1972 and 1976." Presidential Studies Quarter-
        ly 11 (Summer, 1981): 374-83.

        Study of congressional district voting results finds
that Wallace voters along with other Democrats defected to
Nixon in 1972. In 1976 many Wallace backers returned to the
Democrats, but an estimated 5 percent had used a Wallace vote
in 1968 as a step from Democratic to Republican voting behavior.

427.   McEvoy, James, III. "Conservatism or Extremism: Gold-
        water Supporters in the 1964 Presidential Election."
        The American Right Wing: Readings in Political Behav-
        ior (item 443), pp. 241-79.

        Shows that Goldwater supporters were highly educated
and politically involved. Therefore, they do not fit the
extremist stereotype of alienation and low involvement.

428.   _____. Radicals or Conservatives: The Contemporary
        American Right. Chicago: Rand McNally, 1971. 167 pp.

        Empirical analysis concludes that Wallace support
was caused by opposition to civil rights in the South and
support for the use of force against black rioting in the
North. Goldwater and Wallace voters were both protesting
shifting values in society.

429.   Murphy, Reg, and Hal Gulliver. The Southern Strategy.
        New York: Scribner's, 1971. 273 pp.

        Contends that while Nixon delivered on promises made
to southerners, the 1970 election results showed the strategy
to be a failure. Despite the title, the authors suggest that
Nixon's policies were actually a conservative strategy aimed
at the nation.

430.   Oldenick, Robert, and Stephen E. Bennett. "The Wallace
        Factor: Constancy and Cooptation." American Politics
        Quarterly 6 (October, 1978): 460-84.

        Regression analysis of Wallace support in five dif-
ferent years leads to the conclusion that region of sociali-
zation is the most consistently strong explanatory variable.
By 1976, the major parties had absorbed most Wallace voters.

431.   Orum, Anthony M. "Religion and the Rise of the Radi-
        cal White: The Case of Southern Wallace Support in
        1968." Social Science Quarterly 51 (December, 1970):
        674-88.

        On the basis of 207 interviews in the Atlanta area,
Orum discovers that even with education controlled, fundamentalist Baptists supported Wallace more than persons of
other churches because of their beliefs in tradition, asceti-
cism, and individualism.

432.   Page, Benjamin I., and Richard A. Brody. "Policy
        Voting and the Electoral Process: The Vietnam War
        Issue." The American Political Science Review 66
        (September, 1972): 979-95.

        Concludes that policy preferences on the war had a
greater impact on voters' evaluation of Wallace, who was per-
ceived to be the most hawkish candidate, than on their views
of Humphrey and Nixon.

433.   Panetta, Leon E., and Peter Gall. Bring Us Together:
        The Nixon Team and the Civil Rights Retreat. Phila-
        delphia: Lippincott, 1971. 380 pp.

        Former official in HEW's Office of Civil Rights
claims that the Nixon administration modified school desegregation policies to build political support among southern,
pro-Wallace whites.

434.   Peirce, Neal R. The Deep South States of America:
       People, Politics, and Power in the Seven Deep South
       States. New York: Norton, 1974. 528 pp.

       Interview with Thurmond on his meeting with Nixon in
1968 supports the contention that the South Carolinian had
more influence as a Republican than as a Dixiecrat. Wallace,
who used a pugnacious style to defend segregation, also concluded that major party politics offered a greater chance for
respectability and success.

*   _____, and Lawrence D. Longley. The People's Presi-
       dent: The Electoral College in American History and
       the Direct Vote Alternative (item 82)

       Defense of direct vote proposal includes discussion
of the 1968 election. Wallace, who claimed to have swung five
key states to Nixon, told Peirce he would not have allowed the
election to go to the House of Representatives.

435.   "The Public Record of George C. Wallace." Congressional
       Quarterly Weekly Report 26 (September 27, 1968): 2553-
       67.

       Summary of Wallace's political career and policy
views, records that Wallace labelled the Voting Rights Act of
1965 a tragic piece of legislation which should be repealed.

436.   Riesman, David. "The Intellectuals and the Discontented
       Classes: Some Further Reflections-." The Radical
       Right (item 378), pp. 115-34.

       Argues that extremely rapid urbanization and indus-
trialization disrupted southern social structure and made the
region receptive to a leader similar to Joe McCarthy.

437.   Robertson, Wilmot. The Dispossessed Majority. Cape
       Canaveral, Fla.: Howard Allen, 1972. 586 pp.

       Advances the racist notion that the Nordic-Alpine
majority has lost control of America. Wallace achieved a
minor miracle in 1968 with his hard line on racial issues
and the war but failed to restore the majority to power.

438.   Robinson, Michael J., and Clifford Zukin. "Television
         and the Wallace Vote." Journal of Communication 26
         (Spring, 1976): 79-83.

        Discovers relationship between high dependence on
television for political information and voting for Wallace.
Television news conveys an unsettling view of society which
influences well-educated older voters.

439.   Rogin, Michael. "Politics, Emotion and the Wallace
         Vote." The British Journal of Sociology 20 (March,
         1969): 27-49.

        Precinct data and interviews are used to explain
Wallace's 1964 primary strength. Conservatism led to Wallace
votes in Wisconsin and central Indiana while blue-collar
ethnics living close to blacks supplied votes in Gary and
Baltimore.

440.   Roland, Charles P. The Improbable Era: The South
         since World War II. Lexington: University Press of
         Kentucky, 1975. 228 pp.

        Claims that Wallace pulled Nixon closer to southern
views and by 1975 national politics may have adjusted as much
to the South as the reverse.

441.   Ross, J. Michael, Reeve D. Vanneman, and Thomas F. Petti-
         grew. "Patterns of Support for George Wallace: Impli-
         cations for Racial Change." Journal of Social
         Issues 36 (Spring, 1976): 69-91.

        Contends that racial prejudice has been exaggerated
as a source of Wallace strength in the North. Young, lower
middle-class workers were attracted by Wallace's decisiveness
and his attacks on anti-war protesters and government bureaucracy.

442.   St. Angelo, Douglas, and Douglas Dobson. "Candidates,
         Issues, and Political Estrangement: A Research Note
         on 1968 Political Activists." American Politics
         Quarterly 3 (January, 1975): 45-59.

        Study of 265 southern activists identified by bumper-
stickers concludes that Wallace activists were opposed to
national racial policies, conservative on law and order, and
hawkish on Viet Nam.

443.   Schoenberger, Robert A., ed. The American Right Wing:
        Readings in Political Behavior. New York: Holt, Rine-
        hart, and Winston, 1969. 308 pp.

        Introduction by editor notes that far right-wingers
in the 1950's and 1960's stressed their opposition to government bureaucracy and the Soviet Union. Readings on John
Birchers (item 411) and Goldwater supporters (item 427) facil-
itate comparisons with Wallace backers.

444.   _____, and David R. Segal. "The Ecology of Dissent:
        The Southern Wallace Vote in 1968." Midwest Journal
        of Political Science 15 (August, 1971): 583-6.

        Correlation of Wallace vote and socioeconomic vari-
ables in southern congressional districts concludes that
Wallace did better in low-income districts with high percentages of blacks.

445.   Sharkansky, Ira. Regionalism in American Politics.
        Indianapolis, Ind.: Bobbs-Merrill, 1970. 194 pp.

        Provides helpful background against which to evaluate
Wallace's gubernatorial record. Low mass participation and the
power of the conservative while elite has produced low service
levels and regressive tax structures in the South.

446.   Sherrill, Robert. Gothic Politics in the Deep South:
        Stars of the New Confederacy. New York: Grossman,
        1968. 335 pp.

        Describes Thurmond as an individualistic, uncom-
promising defender of conservative, states' rights principles.
Wallace is compared to the Populist Tom Watson, who also
adopted strongly racist views.

447.   Smith, Anita. The Intimate Story of Lurleen Wallace:
        Her Crusade of Courage. Edited by Ron Bigson. Mont-
        gomery, Ala.: Communications Unlimited, 1969. 120
        pp.

        Intensely personal account of Mrs. Wallace's struggle
with cancer notes that she saw her 1966 gubernatorial candidacy as necessary to enable her husband to carry his fight to
the nation in 1968.

448.   Stempel, Guido H., III. "The Prestige Press Meets the
       Third Party Challenge." _Journalism Quarterly_ 46
       (1969): 699-706.

       Concludes that press coverage of the campaign was non-
partisan, but varied greatly in depth of Wallace coverage with
only four of fifteen papers providing treatment equal to that
of the major parties.

449.   Strong, Donald S. "Alabama: Transition and Alienation."
       The Changing Politics of the South (item 412), pp.
       427-71.

       While Wallace symbolized segregation, on non-racial
issues he was a liberal. In 1968, he ran strongly in rural
Alabama and in cities lost only high-income and black precincts.

*   Sundquist, James L. _Dynamics of the Party System: Align-
       ment and Realignment of Political Parties in the United
       States_ (item 109).

       Claims that white opponents of civil rights swung
between major parties and third parties because neither majority
party adopted their position. Wallace ran chiefly on the race
issue which the author expects to fade.

450.   Wallace, George, Jr. _The Wallaces of Alabama: My Fam-
       ily_. As told to James Gregory. Chicago: Follett,
       1975. 256 pp.

       Denies that his father was ever a racist or that his
mother was forced to run for governor. Author advises Democrats to nominate Wallace if they wish to win in 1976.

451.   Warren, Robert, and James J. Best. "The 1968 Election
       in Washington." _The Western Political Quarterly_ 22
       (September, 1969): 536-45.

       Argues that Wallace pulled more votes from Humphrey
than Nixon because the Republican maintained his 1960 strength
in strong Wallace counties.

452.   Wasserman, Ira M. "A Reanalysis of the Wallace Move-
       ment." _Journal of Political and Military Sociology_
       7 (Fall, 1979): 243-56.

       Rejects both the racist and neo-populist explanations
of the Wallace movement and contends that whites were defending

the economic and social benefits which segregation provided
from federal reform efforts.

453.   _____, and David R. Segal. "Aggregation Effects in
        the Ecological Study of Presidential Voting." _Ameri-_
        can Journal of Political Science 17 (February, 1973):
        177-81.

        Modifies the findings of item 82 by use of county-
level data. Percent black correlated positively with the
Wallace vote in the upper South, but negatively in the lower
South because of increased black voting.

454.   Wei, Yung, and H.R. Mahood. "Racial Attitudes and the
        Wallace Vote: A Study of the 1968 Election in Mem-
        phis." _Polity_ 3 (Summer, 1971): 532-49.

        Analysis of 226 Memphis voters before and after the
election identifies attitudes on segregation as the critical
variable linked to a Wallace vote. This finding is valid even
when education and income are controlled.

455.   Weisberg, Herbert F., and Jerrold G. Rusk. "Dimensions
        of Candidate Evaluation." _The American Political_
        Science Review 64 (December, 1970): 1167-85.

        Discovers that Wallace was viewed much more favorably
by persons wishing to use all available force to control urban
unrest than persons supporting other solutions. Party identification played a smaller role with weak Democrats and
independents holding less negative views on Wallace.

456.   White, Theodore H. _The Making of the President, 1968._
        New York: Atheneum, 1969. 459 pp.

        Expresses the view that Wallace was clearly a racist
whose law and order issue was based on white fears of black
violence. The Nixon and Wallace votes are seen as an historic
turn from the promises and experiments of the Johnson Administration.

457.   Wilcox, Allan R., and Leonard B. Weinberg. "Petition-
        Signing in the 1968 Election." _The Western Political_
        Quarterly 24 (December, 1971): 731-9.

        Study of mail questionnaires received from 200 Wal-
lace petition-signers and 600 registered voters reports that

Wallace finished second to Nixon among the signers who helped him obtain ballot position.

458. Winn, Stephen L. "An Analysis of Empirical Research Concerning Electoral Support for George Wallace from 1964 to 1972." Ph.D. dissertation, Washington State University, 1976. 126 pp.

Contends that only education and occupation are consistently related to Wallace support. In 1968, racial prejudice and isolationism differentiated Wallace supporters from Nixon and Humphrey voters.

459. Wright, Gerald C., Jr. "Community Structure and Voting in the South." The Public Opinion Quarterly 40 (Summer, 1976): 201-15.

Concludes that rural white voting for Wallace is more strongly correlated than urban white voting to the level of black concentration. Rural whites seem more fearful of racial violence than urban whites.

460. _____. "Contextual Models of Electoral Behavior: The Southern Wallace Vote." The American Political Science Review 71 (June, 1977): 497-508.

Repeats arguments of item 98 and claims that segregationist campaigns in Deep South states increase Wallace support even in counties with few blacks.

461. Wrinkle, Robert D., and Jerry L. Polinard. "Populism and Dissent: The Wallace Vote in Texas." Social Science Quarterly 54 (December, 1973): 306-20.

Correlation and factor analysis of county-level presidential voting and demographic variables conclude that the Wallace vote is largely explained by urbanism, race, and poverty, and should not be considered populist in nature.

462. _____, and Charles Elliot. "Wallace Party Activists in Texas." Social Science Quarterly 52 (June, 1971): 197-203.

Study of American Independent county chairmen finds them more likely to be fundamentalist Protestants and to have lower incomes than major party chairmen. It is considered unlikely that Wallace activists will obtain leadership roles in the major parties.

CHAPTER 5

THE PROGRESSIVE PARTY

There have been three important political parties in the
United States that have used the name Progressive. Both the
original Progressive Party (1912) and the second Progressive
Party (1924) are rooted in that early twentieth-century reform
movement popularly called progressivism. The third Progressive
Party (1948), however, owed much more to the New Deal than to
progressivism. The similarities between the parties are strik-
ing. Each coalesced around a charismatic leader; each cul-
tivated a liberal, reform ethos; and each failed to endure
despite an auspicious beginning. Nothing demonstrates the
resiliency of the American two-party system more than the
failure of the Progressive parties. Charismatic leadership,
strong issues, and adequate financing proved inadequate to
raise them above the level of temporary phenomena on the American political scene.

PROGRESSIVE PARTY (1912)

The first Progressive Party, often called the "Bull Moose"
Party, was the creation of Theodore Roosevelt. Roosevelt,

109

believing that President William Howard Taft was too conservative, tried to wrest the Republican presidential nomination
away from the incumbent in 1912. Although Roosevelt was far
too popular with the majority of Republicans, Taft controlled
the party machinery and triumphed in the convention. Roosevelt responded to this defeat by allowing his supporters to
form the Progressive Party, and he accepted the new party's
nomination for president.

The platform of the new party, based on Roosevelt's "New
Nationalism," called for direct primaries and direct election
of senators, women's suffrage, income taxes, minimum wages,
prohibition of child labor, health standards for occupations,
and other social and political reforms. On the question of
business, the party supported strong national regulations of
inter-state corporations. This was in keeping with Roosevelt's
view that big business was valuable for its efficiency and
should not be broken up. In total, the Progressive platform
was reformist but certainly not radical.

In the election of 1912, Roosevelt received over four
million votes (27% of the total vote), easily outpolling Taft
and Wilson. On the state and local levels, however, the Progressives fared poorly, demonstrating that the party's appeal
was primarily Roosevelt rather than its positions on the issues

Thus the party failed to attract strong support in the election of 1914 and collapsed entirely in 1916 when Roosevelt returned to the Republicans.

PROGRESSIVE PARTY (1912)

PRIMARY SOURCES

463.   Croly, Herbert. The Promise of American Life. New
        York: Macmillan, 1909. 468 pp.

        This may well be the most influential progressive
work. Theodore Roosevelt borrowed heavily from it in 1912,
even stealing the phrase "the New Nationalism" from Croly.

464.   Pinchot, Amos R. History of the Progressive Party,
        1912-1916. New York: New York University, 1958. 305
        pp. (Edited with a biographical introduction by
        Helene Maxwell Hooker.)

        Prepared from an uncompleted manuscript by Pinchot,
who was a confidant of Theodore Roosevelt and intimately involved with the Progressive Party.

465.   Roosevelt, Theodore. Autobiography. New York: Scrib-
        ner's, 1913. 597 pp.

        Although this is a fairly standard autobiography, it
does contain a fascinating appendix in which Roosevelt defends
himself and the Progressive Party from the charges of being
pro-trust that Woodrow Wilson had levelled during the campaign
of 1912.

466.   _____. The New Nationalism. New York: Outlet Com-
        pany, 1910. 268 pp.

        Excellent collection of Roosevelt's ideas on pro-
gressive reform which formed his basic platform in 1912.

467.   _____. Social Justice and Popular Rule: Essays,
        Addresses and Public Statements Relating to the Pro-
        gressive Movement. New York: Arno, 1974. 578 pp.
        (Reprint of vol. 19 of the Memorial Edition of The
        Works of Theodore Roosevelt, New York: Scribner's,
        1925.)

        This is a collection of Roosevelt's public statements
on Progressivism which provides one with a good perspective on
his views.

468.   Wilson, Woodrow. <u>A Crossroads of Freedom: The 1912</u>
        <u>Campaign Speeches of Woodrow Wilson</u>. New Haven:
        Yale University, 1956. 570 pp. (Edited by John
        Wells Davidson.)

        A complete compendium of Wilson's campaign speeches,
this volume is essential reading for anyone studying the
campaign of 1912.

469.   _____. <u>The New Freedom</u>. New York: Doubleday, 1913.
        294 pp.

        This is Woodrow Wilson's philosophical statement of
Progressivism culled from his many speeches on the subject made
during the campaign of 1912.

SECONDARY SOURCES

470.   Aaron, Daniel. <u>Men of Good Hope: A Story of American</u>
        <u>Progressives</u>. New York: Oxford University, 1961.
        329 pp.

        This study of American reformers includes an interest-
ing chapter on Theodore Roosevelt, whom the author considers
basically conservative.

471.   Abrams, Richard M., ed. <u>The Issues of the Populist</u>
        <u>and Progressive Eras, 1892-1912</u>. Columbia: Univer-
        sity of South Carolina Press, 1969. 283 pp.

        An interesting collection of documents that focuses
most heavily on the issues of the Progressive Era.

472.   Ashby, LeRoy. <u>The Spearless Leader: Senator Borah and</u>
        <u>the Progressive Movement in the 1920's</u>. Urbana:
        University of Illinois, 1972. 325 pp.

        This political biography focuses on the problems of
being a progressive in the twenties and shows how many progressives tried to straddle the political fence during La-
Follette's 1924 campaign.

473.   Bates, James L. <u>The United States, 1898-1928: Pro-</u>
        <u>gressivism and a Society in Transition</u>. New York:
        McGraw-Hill, 1976. 339 pp.

        Excellent introduction to the Progressive Era that con-
tains extremely useful bibliographic essays after each chapter.

474.   Blum, John Morton. The Progressive Presidents: Roose-
       velt, Wilson, Roosevelt, Johnson. New York: Norton,
       Company, 1980. 221 pp.

       The essays on Woodrow Wilson and Theodore Roosevelt
in this book of four essays are quite insightful, especially
in regard to the author's primary interest of presidential
power.

475.   _____. The Republican Roosevelt. Cambridge, Mass.:
       Harvard, 1954. 170 pp.

       A balanced account of Theodore Roosevelt which empha-
sizes his political career and his use of power. Blum demonstrates that Roosevelt's progressivism was unsystematic but
pragmatic.

476.   Bowers, Claude G. Beveridge and the Progressive Era.
       New York: Literary Guild, 1932. 610 pp.

       Much more than a biography, this is a thorough study
of the progressive impulse and of the Progressive Era.

477.   Buenker, John D. Urban Liberalism and Progressive
       Reform. New York: Norton, 1978. 299 pp.

       Buenker argues persuasively that both the urban immi-
grant population and machine politicians supported Progressivism. While this work deals primarily with local politics, it
does raise many interesting points concerning the relationship
among immigrants, machine politicians, and the Democratic Party of Woodrow Wilson.

478.   Chamberlain, John. Farewell to Reform. New York: John
       Day, 1932. 333 pp.

       This is primarily an intellectual study of the pro-
gressive mind which concludes that progressivism was a failure
because it failed to pursue reform thought beyond the point
where such thought became uncomfortable.

479.   Crunden, Robert M. Ministers of Reform: The Progressive
       Achievement in American Civilization. New York: Basic
       Books, 1982. 307 pp.

       This intellectual study of Progressivism attempts to
achieve a new synthesis based on an examination of twenty-one
progressives from various fields.

480. DeWitt, Benjamin Parke. The Progressive Movement.
Seattle: University of Washington, 1968. 376 pp.

Originally published in 1915, this was the first
major study of the Progressive movement, and it has aged well.
While only one chapter is devoted to the Progressive Party,
the whole work is infused with the spirit of progressivism.

481. Ekrich, Arthur A. Progressivism in America. New York:
New Viewpoints, 1974. 308 pp.

Ekrich emphasizes the nationalistic nature of progressivism and details its European roots.

482. Faulkner, Harold U. The Quest for Social Justice,
1898-1914. New York: Macmillan, 1931. 390 pp.

Despite its age, this work still provides an excellent
overview of the early part of the Progressive Era.

483. Filler, Louis. Appointment at Armageddon: Muckraking
and Progressivism in the American Tradition. Westport, Conn.: Greenwood, 1976. 476 pp.

This eccentric study focuses on progressivism as
part of a broader reform tradition which includes muckraking.

484. Gable, John Allen. The Bull Moose Years: Theodore
Roosevelt and the Progressive Party. Port Washington, N.Y.: Kennikat, 1978. 302 pp.

This is the most complete account of the Roosevelt
Progressive Party available, but it is much stronger on description than on analysis.

485. Gardner, Joseph L. Departing Glory: Theodore Roosevelt
as Ex-President. New York: Scribner's, 1973. 432
pp.

This excellent biography of Roosevelt in his later
years is both readable and informative. The section on the
Bull Moose Years is highly entertaining, although not scholarly.

486. Gould, Lewis L., ed. The Progressive Era. Syracuse,
N.Y.: Syracuse University, 1974. 238 pp.

A collection of original essays focusing on both political and intellectual aspects of Progressivism.

487.   _____. Reform and Regulation: American Politics, 1900–
        1916. New York: Wiley, 1978. 197 pp.

        This solid study of the progressive impulse places
the campaign of 1912 within the context of the entire progressive movement.

488.   Graham, Otis L. Encore for Reform: The Old Progressives
        and the New Deal. New York: Oxford, 1967. 256 pp.

        By tracing the activities of a number of progressives
in the New Deal Graham develops a case for the true liberalism
of the Bull Moosers.

489.   _____. The Great Campaigns: Reform and War in Ameri-
        ca, 1900–1928. Englewood Cliffs, N.J.: Prentice-
        Hall, 1971. 386 pp.

        This is an attempt to redefine Progressivism as an
innately conservative movement that sought order just as much
as it sought to help the afflicted in society.

490.   Harbaugh, William H. Power and Responsibility: The
        Life and Times of Theodore Roosevelt. New York:
        Farrar, Straus and Cudahy, 1961. 568 pp.

        This is a solid biography of Roosevelt although the
Progressive Party period is treated only sketchily.

*   Haynes, Fred E. Social Politics in the United States
        (item 45).

        Haynes relates Progressivism to the broader trends
of social reform in the United States. Despite its age, this
work still retains some usefulness in placing progressive
reform into a larger context.

491.   Hays, Samuel P. The Response to Industrialism, 1885–
        1914. Chicago: University of Chicago, 1957. 211 pp.

        This fascinating general study assimilates progressiv-
ism into the mainstream of American culture by demonstrating
that progressivism was only one of the many ways that Americans attempted to cope with a rapidly changing society.

*   Hofstadter, Richard. The Age of Reform (item 54).

        Although this is a study of both Populism and Pro-
gressivism, the sections on the Progressives are much more
convincing. Hofstadter originally propounded the "status revolution" theory of progressivism which is still popular in
some historical circles.

492.   _____, ed. The Progressive Movement, 1900-1915.
        Englewood Cliffs, N.J.: Prentice-Hall, 1963. 185 pp.

        This collection of source materials relating to pro-
gressivism includes the Progressive Party platform of 1912,
Woodrow Wilson's explanation of the "New Freedom," and Theodore Roosevelt's explanation of the "New Nationalism."

493.   Howland, Harold. Theodore Roosevelt and His Times.
        New Haven: Yale University, 1921. 289 pp.

        This dated, but very readable, work devotes several
chapters to the Progressive Party.

494.   Keller, Morton, ed. Theodore Roosevelt: A Profile.
        New York: Hill and Wang, 1967. 194 pp.

        This is a collection of sketches of Roosevelt taken
from previously published sources.

495.   Kennedy, David M. Progressivism: The Critical Issues.
        Boston: Little, Brown, 1971. 191 pp.

        Undistinguished collection of primary and secondary
materials.

496.   Kirby, Jack T. Darkness at the Dawning: Race and Refor-
        mation in the Progressive South. Philadelphia:
        Lippincott, 1972. 210 pp.

        This fascinating book argues that race and progressiv-
ism were interconnected and that segregation was a part of the
progressive reform movement in the South.

497.   Kolko, Gabriel. The Triumph of Conservatism: A Rein-
        terpretation of American History, 1900-1916. New
        York: Free Press, 1963. 344 pp.

        In a major reinterpretation of the progressive impulse
Kolko argues that progressivism was a conservative influence

on society directed by businessmen and politicians determined to ensure the continuity of the capitalist system.

498.   Link, Arthur S. Woodrow Wilson and the Progressive
        Era, 1910-1917. New York: Harper and Row, 1954. 331
        pp.

        While the primary focus of this work is Woodrow Wilson, the opening chapter provides an excellent comparison between Wilson's "New Freedom" and Theodore Roosevelt's "New Nationalism" which were the primary issues in the 1912 election.

499.   Lowitt, Richard. George W. Norris: The Making of a
        Progressive, 1861-1912. Syracuse: Syracuse Univer-
        sity, 1963. 341 pp.

        This is a fine biography of an important Republican progressive. The chapters detailing Norris' campaign for the Senate in 1912 give much insight into the problems faced by progressive Republicans during that time of schism.

500.   Mann, Arthur, ed. The Progressive Era: Liberal Renais-
        sance or Liberal Failure. New York: Holt, Rinehart
        and Winston, 1963. 122 pp.

        A collection of historical essays examining the nature of progressivism and its accomplishments.

501.   May, Henry F. The End of American Innocence: A Study
        of the First Years of Our Own Time, 1912-1917. New
        York: Knopf, 1959. 430 pp.

        Although there is only a smattering of material on progressivism in this book, it is still one of the finest studies of the period, especially in terms of literature and culture.

502.   Mowry, George E. The California Progressives. Chicago:
        Quadrangle, 1963. 344 pp.

        Although primarily concerned with California, this work is an important source of insight into progressive attitudes and motivations.

503. _____. The Era of Theodore Roosevelt, 1900-1912. New
        York: Harper and Row, 1958. 330 pp.

      A solid and readable study of Theodore Roosevelt's
ideas and actions, this work contains an excellent account of
the events leading up to Roosevelt's decision to run as third-
party candidate in 1912.

504. _____. The Progressive Era, 1900-1920: The Reform
        Persuasion. Washington: American Historical Associa-
        tion, 1972. 39 pp.

      This slim volume contains a good summary of progres-
sivism and a brief account of the high points of progressive
historiography.

505. _____. Theodore Roosevelt and the Progressive Move-
        ment. Madison: University of Wisconsin, 1946. 405
        pp.

      This is the premier account of the events leading up
to the creation of the Progressive Party in 1912. So much
detail is present about the years 1909-1912 that the section
on the Progressive Party itself seems almost an afterthought.

506. Noble, David. The Paradox of Progressive Thought.
        Minneapolis: University of Minnesota, 1958. 272 pp.

      Noble examines the ideas of several progressive in-
tellectuals including Herbert Croly, Richard Ely, and Walter
Rauschenbusch so as to elucidate the progressive world view.

*   Nye, Russel B. Midwestern Progressive Politics: A
        Historical Study of Its Origins and Development, 1870-
        1950 (item 80).

      Despite the title, this thorough study of American
reform is extremely valuable to all students of progressivism.
Nye quite convincingly demonstrates the connections between
earlier reform movements and progressivism.

507. Pease, Otis A., ed. The Progressive Years: The Spirit
        and Achievement of American Reform. New York: Brazil-
        ler, 1962. 496 pp.

      A very well selected collection of documents relating
to progressivism which is distinguished by lacking the severe
editing that mars many works of this type.

508.   Pringle, Henry F. Theodore Roosevelt: A Biography.
        New York: Harcourt, Brace, 1931. 627 pp.

        This, the standard biography of Roosevelt, is ex-
haustive and objective, and it has stood up well to the years.

509.   Southern, David W. The Malignant Heritage: Yankee Pro-
        gressives and the Negro Question, 1901-1914. Chicago:
        Loyola University, 1968. 116 pp.

        The author argues that northern progressives never
really extended their reform impulse towards the black portion
of their society.

510.   Tager, Jack. The Intellectual as Urban Reformer: Brand
        Whitlock and the Progressive Movement. Cleveland:
        Case Western Reserve, 1968. 198 pp.

        Solid study of one of the most fascinating members of
the progressive movement.

511.   Timberlake, James H. Prohibition and the Progressive
        Movement. Cambridge, Mass.: Harvard University, 1963.
        238 pp.

        The author relates the prohibition movement of the
Progressive Era to a middle-class effort to regain control of
society. Strangely, given the widespread acceptance of the
"status revolution" theory of progressivism (item 54), the
author does little to tie the two movements together.

512.   Weinstein, James. The Corporate Ideal in the Liberal
        State: 1900-1918. Boston: Beacon Press, 1968. 263
        pp.

        In the very perceptive chapter on the Progressive
Party of 1912, the author maintains that any difference between
the parties was almost purely rhetorical.

513.   Wiebe, Robert H. Businessmen and Reform: A Study of
        the Progressive Movement. Cambridge, Mass.: Harvard
        University, 1962. 283 pp.

        An examination of the conservative contributions of
businessmen to the ideology of progressivism. The author notes
that Roosevelt received little active support from business in
1912.

514.   Wilson, R. Jackson, ed. Reform, Crisis, and Confusion,
        1900-1929. New York: Random House, 1970. 210 pp.

        A good collection of excerpts from important studies
of Progressivism, this work serves as an excellent introduction
to the historiography of the period.

BIBLIOGRAPHIES

515.   Buenker, John D. Progressive Reform: A Guide to Infor-
        mation Sources. Detroit: Gale Research, 1980. 366 pp.

        Broad bibliographic examination of all aspects of the
Progressive Era.

516.   Filler, Louis. Progressivism and Muckraking. New York:
        Bowker, 1976. 200 pp.

        This is an extended bibliographic essay which looks
at reform in America from the beginning of the twentieth century
to the present. While far from exhaustive, it is a very useful work.

PROGRESSIVE PARTY (1924)

The revival of the Progressive Party in 1924 was the work

of Senator Robert M. LaFollette of Wisconsin. LaFollette, a

reform-minded Republican for most of his career, had opposed

the creation of a separate party in 1912 because it would give

control of the Republican Party to its conservative element.

Events proved his analysis to be correct, and by 1924 the Re-

publicans were far more conservative than they had been in

1912. LaFollette, in a desperate attempt to revive the reform

movement, bolted the party and tried to unify the old reform

elements in a new Progressive Party.

The Progressive platform in 1924 was considerably more radical than that of 1912. It called for government ownership of the railroads, direct nomination and election of the President, abolition of the use of injunctions in labor strikes, and Congressional override of Supreme Court decisions. The Progressives also reiterated their traditional stand against unfettered monopolies and called for lower tariffs. Unlike 1912 when all of the major parties claimed some degree of progressivism, the Progressives of 1924 were clearly the most radical of the seriously contending parties.

Repeating the mistake of 1912, the Progressives concentrated their campaign on the national level rather than trying to develop state and local organizations. Thus the party, which obtained almost five million votes (16% of the total vote), was unable to build upon this strength for the future. Indeed, LaFollette's death in 1925 ended the party's effectiveness, for only he had been able to hold together the labor, agrarian, liberal, and Socialist factions that made up the Progressive coalition.

PRIMARY SOURCES

517.   Croly, Herbert. "LaFollette." New Republic 40 (October 1924): 221-24.

   This brief article is interesting in that Croly, the intellectual articulator of the progressive program, affirms his support for LaFollette while criticizing him for not reaching beyond middle-class reform.

518.   LaFollette, Robert M. LaFollette's Autobiography. 3rd edition. Madison, Wisc.: Robert M. LaFollette, 1919. 807 pp.

   LaFollette intended this work to be a campaign document in his bid for the Republican presidential nomination in 1912. It elucidates LaFollette's progressive ideals and scathingly attacks Theodore Roosevelt's progressive credentials.

519.   Torrelle, Ellen, ed. The Political Philosophy of Robert M. LaFollette. Madison, Wisc.: LaFollette, 1920.

   A compendium of LaFollette documents and speeches designed to portray his positions on political and social questions.

SECONDARY SOURCES

520.   Doan, Edward N. The LaFollettes and the Wisconsin Idea. New York: Rinehart, 1947. 311 pp.

   This generally unsatisfactory work provides little illumination on the campaign of 1924.

521.   Greenbaum, Fred. Robert Marion LaFollette. Boston: Twayne, 1975. 275 pp.

   Unexceptional but well-written biography which barely touches upon the 1924 campaign.

522.   LaFollette, Belle Case, and Fola LaFollette. Robert M. LaFollette: June 14, 1855-June 18, 1925. New York: Macmillan, 1953. 1305 pp.

   Although written by his wife and daughter and therefore somewhat uncritical, this biography contains a wealth of material about LaFollette's life and political thought.

523.   Link, Arthur S. "What Happened to the Progressive Move-
          ment in the 1920's?" American Historical Review 64
          (July 1959): 836-51.

          This article provides lucid explanations for LaFol-
lette's failure to become a serious threat to the established
parties in 1924.

524.   MacKay, Kenneth C. The Progressive Movement of 1924.
          New York: Octagon, 1972. 298 pp.

          This is a detailed and thoughtful account of LaFol-
lette's campaign in 1924. The concluding chapter is an especially succinct analysis of the problems facing third parties.

525.   Maney, Patrick J. "Young Bob" LaFollette: A Biography
          of Robert M. LaFollette, Jr., 1895-1953. Columbia:
          University of Missouri, 1978. 338 pp.

          The first chapters have some material on LaFollette,
Senior, including a brief account of the 1924 campaign.

526.   Maxwell, Robert H. LaFollette and the Rise of the Pro-
          gressives in Wisconsin. Madison: State Historical
          Society of Wisconsin, 1956. 271 pp.

          Although this work is primarily concerned with Wis-
consin and does not cover the 1924 campaign, it is a valuable
examination of the development of LaFollette's political and
social thought.

527.   Thelan, David P. Robert M. LaFollette and the Insur-
          gent Spirit. Boston: Little, Brown, 1976. 211 pp.

          An excellent political biography based upon the LaFol-
lette papers. Only one chapter is devoted to the presidential
campaign of 1924, but considerable attention is given to La-
Follette's relations with Roosevelt, Wilson, and other Progressives.

PROGRESSIVE PARTY (1948)

Henry A. Wallace had served as Secretary of Agriculture, Secretary of Commerce, and Vice President of the United States. (1941-45) when he decided in 1948 to form a new party. Long a proponent of improving American relations with the Soviet Union, Wallace had convinced himself that Harry Truman's anti-Soviet policies were leading to another global conflict. He therefore offered himself to the nation as a candidate of peace representing the new Progressive Party.

As a peace party, the Progressive platform emphasized foreign policy. It called for an end to the Marshall Plan, for the elimination of universal military training, and for the United States to work with the Soviet Union towards disarmament. The platform also called for the creation of a world government under the auspices of the United Nations. The radicalism of these planks exposed the Progressives to charges of communist domination which seriously hurt their campaign.

In domestic affairs the Progressives espoused such unpopular ideas as racial integration, the legalization of the Communist Party, the repeal of the Taft-Hartley Act, and the abolition of the House Committee on Un-American Activities. The party also favored such standard reforms as the extension of Social Security, increased regulation of monopolies, increased welfare legislation, and the nationalization of utilities. These ideals were also branded by many as communist-inspired.

When Wallace was endorsed by the Communist Party of the United States and failed to disavow the endorsement, many voters apparently concluded that the charges against the Progressives had some substance. Thus Wallace garnered only a little over a million votes (2%) in the election with almost half of them coming from New York. This electoral failure marked the effective end of the Progressive Party, although it did run a candidate for President in 1952.

PRIMARY SOURCES

528.   Baldwin, C.B. "Wallace's Campaign Manager Replies to Gardner Jackson." Atlantic 182 (August 1948): 16-19.

        Baldwin, Wallace's campaign manager, sets out Wallace' program and argues that the new party wants to develop a "progressive" capitalism by curbing monopoly and other bad aspects of the existing "reactionary" capitalistic system.

529.   Wallace, Henry A. The Century of the Common Man. New York: Reynal and Hitchcock, 1943. 96 pp.

        A collection of Wallace's speeches as Vice President.

530.   _____. New Frontiers. New York: Reynal and Hitchcock, 1934. 314 pp.

        A defense of the New Deal and an early exposition of Wallace's view of the need for social cooperation to solve economic problems.

531.   _____. The Price of Vision: The Diary of Henry A.
            Wallace, 1942-46. Edited by John Morton Blum. Boston:
            Houghton Mifflin, 1973. 707 pp.

        This is an important document that covers the period
in which most of Wallace's campaign ideas on foreign policy
were developed. The introduction by Blum is excellent.

532.   _____. Sixty Million Jobs. New York: Reynal and Hitch-
            cock, 1945. 216 pp.

        While still Secretary of Commerce Wallace wrote this
book to propose that government assume the responsibility for
providing full employment through planning, taxation, and
resource development. Many of his campaign proposals appear
here in a less politicized form.

533.   _____. Statesmanship and Religion. London: Williams
            and Norgate, 1934. 139 pp.

        This little book is a statement of Wallace's faith and
idealism which provides a great deal of insight into the
strength of character that would lead him into revolt against
the established political parties.

534.   _____. Toward World Peace. New York: Reynal and
            Hitchcock, 1948. 121 pp.

        This is Wallace's campaign book, and it is the crucial
document to understanding Wallace's views and positions in 1948.

*   _____. "Why a Third Party in 1948?" Annals of the
            American Academy of Political and Social Science
            (item 114).

        Wallace explains both the role of the third party in
American politics and his goals for the Progressive Party.

                        SECONDARY SOURCES

535.   Hald, William H. "What Makes Wallace Run?" Harper's
            186 (March 1948): 241-48.

        This is a fascinating look at the background of
Wallace's decision to run for the presidency in 1948 which,
although critical, is much more generous to Wallace than are
most contemporary accounts of his candidacy.

536.   Jackson, Gardner. "Henry Wallace: A Divided Mind."
        Atlantic 182 (August 1948): 27-33.

        This is an attack on Wallace which accuses him of
being soft on communism and of trying to swing the election to
the Republicans by diverting votes from Truman.

537.   Lord, Russell. The Wallaces of Iowa. Boston: Houghton,
        Mifflin, 1947. 615 pp.

        This book is valuable in that it looks at Wallace's
family and agricultural background, and as such it enables the
student to understand better Wallace's controversial nature.

538.   MacDonald, Dwight. Henry Wallace: The Man and the Myth.
        New York: Vanguard Press, 1948. 187 pp.

        This attack on Wallace's political and foreign policy
positions appeared during the 1948 campaign. However biased
MacDonald might have been, he still presented a strong case
against Wallace.

539.   MacDougall, Curtis D. Gideon's Army. New York: Marzoni
        and Munsell, 1965. 2 volumes. 586 pp.

        This massive work contains some questionable scholar-
ship, but it also contains a wealth of data: about Wallace's
campaign for the presidency in 1948.

540.   Markowitz, Norman D. The Rise and Fall of the People's
        Century: Henry A. Wallace and American Liberalism,
        1941-48. New York: Free Press, 1973. 369 pp.

        This is probably the best study of Wallace's mind
which manages to convey in a sympathetic and objective manner
the contradictions in his thinking which led Wallace to attempt
to combine socialism and capitalism in one system.

541.   Ross, Irwin. The Loneliest Campaign: The Truman Victory
        of 1948. New York: New American Library, 1968.

        This is a journalistic rather than scholarly account
of the election of 1948. The author gives more attention to
the major party candidates than to Wallace.

542.   Schapsmeier, Edward L., and Frederick H. Schapsmeier.
        Prophet in Politics: Henry A. Wallace and the War
        Years, 1940-1965. Ames: Iowa State University, 1970.
        268 pp.

        While excellent for background on Wallace's views,
this biography has only one surprisingly sketchy chapter on the
presidential campaign of 1948.

543.   Schmidt, Karl M. Henry A. Wallace: Quixotic Crusade
        1948. Syracuse, N.Y.: Syracuse University, 1960.
        362 pp.

        Heavily based on personal interviews, this is a
thorough and balanced account of the Progressive Party of 1948.

544.   Walker, J. Samuel. Henry A. Wallace and American
        Foreign Policy. Westport, Conn.: Greenwood, 1976.
        224 pp.

        Heavily based on the Wallace papers, this is an ex-
haustive and discerning account of Wallace's beliefs concerning American foreign policy. The chapter about Wallace's campaign in 1948, however, is disappointingly brief.

545.   Walton, Richard J. Henry Wallace, Harry Truman, and
        the Cold War. New York: Viking, 1976. 388 pp.

        This is an intelligent study of the foreign policy
problems between Wallace and Truman that led to Wallace's Progressive campaign for the presidency in 1948 and the debate
over American-Soviet relations that developed during the campaign.

546.   Yarnell, Allen. Democrats and Progressives: The 1948
        Presidential Election as a Test of Postwar Liberalism.
        Berkeley: University of California, 1974.

        Yarnell argues that the Progressive Party failed in
that it was unable to win Democratic acceptance of its ideas.

CHAPTER 6

MINOR THIRD PARTIES

Minor third parties represent the fringes of the political
spectrum, regional concerns, or single issue groups. Few conduct campaigns on a national scale, and even fewer have influenced the outcome of national elections. The parties represented in this chapter, however, did make some attempt to
develop national followings and are therefore of interest to
social and political historians.

PROHIBITION PARTY

The Prohibition Party began in response to the Republican
and Democratic parties' refusal to support a prohibition plank,
and it has fielded candidates in every presidential election
since 1872. Although the major issue of the party has always
been the prohibition of the manufacture, sale, and consumption
of alcohol, it has also advocated issues as diverse as suffrage
for women, direct election of senators, a federal income tax,
and conservation of natural resources. The party reached its
peak of popular support in the 1892 election, when it received
over 2 percent of the popular vote.

Ironically, the Prohibition Party is considered only a peripheral influence in the temperance movement and the passage of the Prohibition Amentment. Other nonpartisan groups, notably the Anti-Saloon League and the Women's Christian Temperance Union, were the major influences behind the movement's success. The present day party appeals primarily to church groups and older persons who share the party's advocacy of a return to more fundamental moral values.

SOURCES

547.   Blocker, Jack S., Jr. <u>Retreat from Reform: The Pro-</u>
       <u>hibition Movement in the United States, 1880-1913</u>.
       Westport, Conn.: Greenwood, 1976. 261 pp.

       Detailed history of Prohibition Party and its relation-
ship with other temperance organizations. Traces party's
internal struggles between fusionist and anti-fusionist factions, and the broad-gauge versus narrow-gauge debate. Extensive coverage of party conventions and publications.

548.   Byrne, Frank Loyola. <u>Prophet of Prohibition: Neal Dow</u>
       <u>and his Crusade</u>. Madison, Wisc.: State Historical
       Society of Wisconsin, 1961. 184 pp.

       Chronicles life of early prohibitionist and author of
the Maine law. Dow became a leader and candidate of the newly
formed Prohibition Party.

549.   Clark, Norman. <u>Deliver Us from Evil: An Interpretation</u>
       <u>of American Prohibition</u>. New York: Norton, 1976. 246
       pp.

       Excellent, in-depth account of prohibition from early
colonial times through repeal. Explores factors of industrialization, westward expansion, and increased foreign immigration and their relationship to the prohibition movement.
Clark argues prohibition was a traditional reform movement,
not a prolonged exercise in repression.

550.   Colvin, David Leigh. <u>Prohibition in the United States</u>:
       <u>A History of the Prohibition Party, and of the Pro-</u>
       <u>hibition Movement</u>. New York: Doran, 1926. 678 pp.

       Thorough account of party formation in context of
general temperance movement, includes campaign platforms and
biographical material. Written by leading party activist and
former vice-presidential candidate, Colvin's history reflects
strong partisan bias.

551.   Gusfield, Joseph R. <u>Symbolic Crusade: Status Politics</u>
       <u>and the American Temperance Movement</u>. Urbana, Ill.:
       University of Illinois Press, 1963. 198 pp.

       This work offers a sociological interpretation of the
temperance movement. Gusfield views the prohibitionists'
ostensible goal of enforced abstinence as a symbol of their

actual goal—to use the issue of moral reform to enhance
their group's social status. Although the work offers very
little new historical data, its application of the theory of
status conflict to the temperance movement adds significantly
to our understanding of the prohibitionists.

552.   Kobler, John.   Ardent Spirits, The Rise and Fall of
        Prohibition.   New York: Putnam, 1973.   386 pp.

        Thorough coverage of prohibition history using per-
sonal accounts and primary source material.

553.   Storms, Roger C.   Partisan Prophets: A History of the
        Prohibition Party, 1854-1972.   Denver: National Pro-
        hibition Foundation, 1972.   71 pp.

        Concise history written by active party member chron-
icles party development over three distinct periods: broad-
gauge platform, narrow-gauge platform, and present day call to
return to fundamental moral values. Largely biographical
sketches of party leaders.

*   Timberlake, James H.   Prohibition and the Progressive
        Movement.   Cambridge, Mass.: Harvard University, 1963
        (item 511).

        An examination of the principal arguments of the pro-
hibitionists and the basic nature of their political support.

GREENBACK PARTY

        The Greenback Party was an outgrowth of the Grange move-

ment and represents a link between the Grangers and the Popu-

lists. Entering national politics in the presidential cam-

paign of 1876 with New York philanthropist Peter Cooper as its

candidate, the party was only able to achieve eighty thousand

votes. After a strong showing in 1878, electing congressmen

and polling over a million votes (including fusion candidates),

the party ran James B. Weaver for president in 1881 but received only 300,000 votes. It rapidly faded from the political

scene after 1880, although many of its personalities and issues

came to prominence during the Populist revolt of the 1890's.

Primarily a midwestern movement, the Greenback Party plat-

form was predicated on economic unrest. Equating deflation

with economic depression, the Greenbackers wanted the govern-

ment to inflate the money supply by issuing paper currency

that was not backed by gold. Eventually, many Greenback

supporters shifted their inflationary hopes to silver and their

political support to the People's Party.

Despite its brief prominence, the Greenback Party has

been relegated to obscurity by historians who have concen-

trated primarily on its direct descendent--Populism.

SOURCES

554.   Buck, Solon J. The Agrarian Crusade, A Chronicle of
         the Farmer in Politics. New Haven: Yale University,
         1920. 215 pp.

Contains an excellent chapter on the Greenback movement, placing it in relation to both the Granger and Populist
movements.

*   Haynes, Fred E. Third Party Movements since the Civil
         War with Special Reference to Iowa (item 46).

Haynes is especially informative on the Greenback
movement, although much of his work is now somewhat dated.

*   Nugent, Walter T.K. The Money Question During Recon-
             struction (item 169).

         Excellent background material for developing an under-
standing of the Greenback Party's monetary views.

555.   Unger, Irwin. The Greenback Era: A Social and Politi-
             cal History of American Finance, 1865-1879. Prince-
             ton, N.J.: Princeton University, 1964. 467 pp.

         This is the definitive work on the history of the
Greenback Party.

                        UNION PARTY--1936

         The Union Party was organized in the spring of 1936 by

Father Charles Coughlin of Detroit as a protest against the

New Deal policies of Franklin Roosevelt. Coughlin, an advo-

cate of a central bank and enlarged money supply, hoped to

unite the members of his National Union for Social Justice

with the supporters of Francis Townsend's plan for old-age

pensions and hard-pressed farmers attracted by debt relief

proposals.

         Coughlin chose William Lemke, a North Dakota Republican

congressman, as the party's presidential candidate. Both

Coughlin and Lemke had been Roosevelt supporters before con-

cluding that the New Deal was not sufficiently radical to

alleviate the economic problems of the time.

         In the election, Lemke won just under 2 percent of the

popular vote, as many Coughlin and Townsend followers remained loyal to Roosevelt. Lack of coordination among the party's discordant leaders and failure to gain ballot access in twelve states including California have been identified as factors which limited the party's success.

SOURCES

556.   Bennett, David H. Demagogues in the Depression: Ameri-
        can Radicals and the Union Party, 1932-1936. New
        Brunswick, N.J.: Rutgers University Press, 1969.
        341 pp.

        Presents a more thorough account of the Union Party
than other works which focus on the party's individual leaders.
Author finds Coughlin and Smith more demagogic than Lemke and
Townsend, but sees a common reliance on monetary panaceas to
resolve the problems of the elderly, farmers, and German and
Irish Catholics.

557.   Blackorby, Edward C. Prairie Rebel: The Public Life of
        William Lemke. Lincoln: University of Nebraska Press,
        1963. 339 pp.

        Thorough review of the career of the Union Party's
candidate concludes that his third party venture was a mistake which detracted from his advocacy of justice for American farmers. The author utilizes both the Lemke papers and
interviews.

558.   Brinkley, Alan. Voices of Protest: Huey Long, Father
        Coughlin, and the Great Depression. New York: Knopf,
        1982. 348 pp.

        Argues that Long and Coughlin were protesting threats
to individual freedom created by the modern industrial state.
The protesters' strength had declined by the 1936 election
because of Long's death, the "Second" New Deal and the refusal
of many Coughlin followers to reject Roosevelt.

559.   Burns, James MacGregor. <u>Roosevelt: The Lion and the</u>
        <u>Fox</u>. New York: Harcourt, Brace, 1956. 553 pp.

        Holds that the appeal of radical leaders rested on
the desire of millions not yet helped by complex New Deal
programs for simple solutions to their economic miseries.

560.   Coughlin, Charles E. <u>A Series of Lectures on Social</u>
        <u>Justice</u>. 1935 Reprint. New York: Da Capo, 1971.
        244 pp.

        Contains collection of speeches from November, 1934,
to March, 1935, by the "radio priest" who later became the
driving force for the Union Party. Speeches criticize the
New Deal for compromising with bankers and industrialists.

561.   Holtzman, Abraham. <u>The Townsend Movement: A Political</u>
        <u>Study</u>. New York: Bookman Associates, 1963. 256 pp.

        Credits the Townsend movement for pensions with in-
creasing the self-consciousness of older Americans. Brief
treatment of Townsend's support of the Union Party contends
that it weakened the movement. Support for monetary panaceas
is cited as evidence of the conservatism of some American
radicals.

562.   McCoy, Donald R. <u>Angry Voices: Left-of-Center Politics</u>
        <u>in the New Deal Era</u>. Lawrence: University of Kansas
        Press, 1958. 224 pp.

        The formation of the Union Party is considered a re-
sult of the decision of more responsible farmer-labor leaders
not to organize a progressive party after 1929 and especially
in a May 1936 convention.

563.   Marcus, Sheldon. <u>Father Coughlin: The Tumultuous Life</u>
        <u>of the Priest of the Little Flower</u>. Boston: Little,
        Brown, 1973. 317 pp.

        Attributes split with Roosevelt to Coughlin's dis-
approval of New Deal economic policies and his failure to become a close presidential advisor. Lemke was chosen as candidate because he would not overshadow Coughlin. Author finds
that the priest's memory in interviews is not always supported
by historical data.

*   Schlesinger, Arthur M., Jr. The Age of Roosevelt: The
        Politics of Upheaval. Boston: Houghton, Mifflin,
        1960 (item 224).

        Three chapters picture Coughlin, Long, and Townsend
as demagogues attacking Roosevelt from the left. The poor
showing of the Union Party is attributed to its extreme rhetoric and the incompatibility of its leaders.

564.   Tull, Charles J. Father Coughlin and the New Deal.
        Syracuse: Syracuse University Press, 1965. 292 pp.

        Summarizes Coughlin's career and his role in helping
organize the Union Party. Author relies primarily on Coughlin's published speeches, and material from Roosevelt administration sources.

LIBERTARIAN PARTY

The Libertarian Party espouses a philosophy of individual

liberty and economic freedom from government regulation. The

party, founded in 1972, traces its heritage back to the found-

ing fathers and their ideas of limited government and personal

freedom. Attacking both liberals and conservatives, Liber-

tarians believe that the only role of government is to defend

individuals from violence, aggression, and fraud. With organi-

zations in all fifty states, the Libertarian Party is repre-

sented in hundreds of state and local elections, as well as in

presidential races. In the election of 1980, Edward W. Clark,

the Libertarian candidate for president, polled over 900,000

votes.

SOURCES

565.   Clark, Ed. <u>A New Beginning</u>. Aurora, Ill.: Caroline
        House, 1980. 135 pp.

        1980 Libertarian Party presidential candidate's pro-
gram for change. Presents political philosophy and proposals
for wide range or issues including foreign policy, the economy,
the military, etc. Offers specific criticism of Reagan,
Carter, and Anderson campaign promises.

566.   Crane, Ed. "America's Third Largest Party: Success!"
        <u>Reason</u> 9(4)(August 1977): 15-18.

        Refutes Royce's article (item 573) and defends Liber-
tarian Party as a viable political alternative and useful ve-
hicle to promote Libertarian philosophy. Examines party's
success at the polls.

567.   deRosa, Peter. "Where They Stand: The Libertarian Par-
        ty and Its Competition, 1968-1978." <u>Journal of Lib-
        ertarian Studies</u> 3(4) 1979: 391-403.

        Comparison of third party vote totals for six national
elections, with particular emphasis on Libertarian Party results.

568.   Hospers, John. <u>Libertarianism: A Political Philosophy
        for Tomorrow</u>. Los Angeles: Nash Publishing, 1971.
        488 pp.

        Former Libertarian Party presidential candidate pre-
sents party's conservative philosophy of the relationship between government and liberty and individual rights. Argues
for limited government in role of protective agency.

569.   Judis, John. "Libertarianism: Where the Left Meets
        the Right." <u>Progressive</u> 44 (September 1980): 36-38.

        Overview of party philosophy and divergent left-
leaning and right-leaning groups within the party, specifically
in light of 1980 election. Author critical of economic aims
and libertarian belief in ability of private sector to remedy
national economic problems.

570.   MacBride, Roger L. A New Dawn for America: The Liber-
       tarian Challenge. Ottawa, Ill.: Green Hill, 1976.
       111 pp.

       Party's 1976 candidate outlines a program to end
government control of the money supply, abolish regulatory
agencies, return to a non-interventionist foreign policy, and
eliminate laws against victimless crime.

571.   Nelson, Michael. "The New Libertarians: Stripping
       Government of Its Powers." Saturday Review 7 (1
       March 1980): 21-24.

       Brief history of party and its objectives, including
biographical sketches of party leaders. Author argues Libertarian Party is real third-party alternative, although he is
skeptical of their desire to abolish government.

572.   Rothbard, Murray. For a New Liberty. Revised edition.
       New York: Collier, 1978. 338 pp.

       Leading Libertarian economist and party member traces
Libertarian heritage from western Europe to its roots in
founding of U.S. Lengthy review of Libertarian tenets and
proposals for solving current major problems espouses views of
left-wing Libertarians.

573.   Royce, E. Scott. "America's Third Largest Party:
       Failure!" Reason 9 (4), (August 1977): 14, 19-23.

       Author contends Libertarian Party is not viable alter-
native in two-party system based on totals in recent elections.
Suggests party transform itself into non-partisan grassroots
political action group recruiting and supporting candidates
committed to Libertarian program.

                     EUGENE J. MCCARTHY

       Eugene J. McCarthy, former Democratic Senator from Minne-

sota, twice sought his party's nomination for President. In

1976, he made his third bid for the presidency as the nominee

of the independent Committee for a Constitutional Presidency.

Campaigning on a platform that called for reductions in military expenditures, restrictions on the intelligence agencies, a return to idealism in foreign policy, reduced American consumption of natural resources, and increased emphasis on ending poverty, McCarthy sought to provide the American people with a liberal alternative to the existing parties. Ineligible for federal funding and able to obtain a place on the ballot in only twenty-nine states, however, McCarthy received only 1 percent of the popular vote.

PRIMARY SOURCES

574.   McCarthy, Eugene. "It Is a Closed System, and One
       Suspects It Was Meant to Be Closed." Center Magazine
       8 (November 1975): 20-22.

       Citing discrimination, violation of Constitutional rights and perpetuation of two-party system, McCarthy protests new campaign financing act.

575.   _____. "Sins of Omission." Harper's 254 (June 1977):
       90-92.

       Accuses media of unequal campaign coverage based on arbitrary determination of candidates' significance, specifically in 1976 presidential race.

SECONDARY SOURCES

576.   Alexander, Herbert E. Financing the 1976 Election.
       Washington, D.C.: Congressional Quarterly, 1979,
       pp. 434-55.

       Discussion of fund-raising restrictions and ballot access problems faced by McCarthy; also disclosure of campaign spending.

577.   Bode, Ken. "The McCarthy Factor." New Republic 175
          (October 23, 1976): 10-12.

        Claiming a vote for McCarthy equals a vote for Ford,
Carter and party leaders urge Democrats to toe party line.

578.   _____. "McCarthy's Quest." New Republic 175 (July
          3, 1976): 7+.

        Reviews ballot access restrictions and discusses how
system impedes independent challenges.

579.   Brower, Brock. "Lean, Mean Gene." New York Times,
          October 24, 1976, section 6, p. 12+.

        McCarthy, still identified with protest campaign of
1968, offers reasons for running as independent.

580.   Castelli, Jim. "Digging Up the Rose Garden: McCarthy
          Challenges the System." Nation 221 (August 30, 1975):
          142-45.

        Strategy of McCarthy campaign to appeal to nonvoters,
liberals, and independents and prove dissatisfaction with
major parties and institution of presidency.

581.   Chu, Daniel. "McCarthy On His Own." Newsweek 88
          (November 1976): 24.

        McCarthy rails against imperial presidency and closed
political system, leaving Democrats to worry about his influence on Carter victory.

*   Einsiedel, E.F., and J.M. Bibbee. "The News Magazines
          and Minority Candidates--Campaign '76" (item 34).

        Study of three major news magazines proves coverage
of McCarthy campaign unbiased but very limited, questions
effect on voting behavior.

582.   "Election Re-Cap." Gallup Opinion Index 137 (December
          1976): 13-19.

        Polls show McCarthy's popular support, group break-
down of support, and effects of vote switching on final tally.

583.   Jones, Rochelle. "McCarthy: Calling for New Electoral
        Process." Congressional Quarterly Weekly Report 33
        (October 25, 1975): 2279-83.

        Overview of McCarthy campaign, including position on
issues and efforts to overcome restrictions of new election
laws and two-party monopoly.

584.   "McCarthy Says He Doesn't Care If His Votes Help Re-
        Elect Ford. We Do." New Republic 175 (October 30,
        1976): 4; Nation 223 (October 30, 1976): 440.

        Former 1968 McCarthy supporters urge voters not to
risk Ford victory by voting for McCarthy in full-page adver-
tisement authorized and paid for by 1976 Democratic Presidential Campaign.

585.   Whittemore, Reed. "The Case for McCarthy." Common-
        weal 103 (October 22, 1976): 686+.

        McCarthy's objectives to unfreeze two-party monopoly,
return foreign policy responsibility to Congress, restore
integrity of government institutions.

586.   "Will Gene Be the Spoiler?" Time 108 (October 25, 1976):
        17-18.

        McCarthy names prospective cabinet; Carter campaign
concerned about independent's impact on close-finish election.

587.   Witcover, Jules. "Reports and Comment: Campaigning."
        Atlantic 236 (September 1975): 12-14.

        McCarthy's iconoclastic style resurfaces in low-key
independent bid for presidency.

                         JOHN ANDERSON

    John Anderson, originally a conservative Republican

Congressman from Illinois, became a moderate Republican in

response to Watergate, the Vietnam War, and the civil rights

movement. Dissatisfied with his role as a minority voice in a minority party, Anderson sought the Republican presidential nomination in 1980. Although he attracted some attention, it became apparent to Anderson that his true appeal was to Democrats and independent voters, and he decided to campaign for the presidency as an independent candidate.

Anderson's platform was a combination of fiscal conservatism and social liberalism. On the one hand he favored legal abortion, the Equal Rights Amendment, gun control, and nuclear arms reduction, while on the other hand he endorsed balancing the budget through the reduction of government spending. One of his most controversial proposals was a fifty-cent per gallon tax on gasoline to encourage conservation and lessen American dependence on foreign oil. The mixture of conservatism and liberalism that characterized both Anderson and his platform confused voters and made his already formidable task as an independent even more difficult.

Anderson's campaign lacked funds and local party organizations, and his inexperienced campaign staff had to devote considerable effort to ballot-access drives. These drawbacks made it difficult for Anderson to convince voters that he was a viable candidate, and a lack of media coverage made it even more difficult for him. Even a nationally televised debate with Ronald Reagan failed to bolster Anderson's candidacy.

In the election Anderson finished a poor third with

approximately 7 percent of the popular vote. While the results

were disappointing to Anderson, he did manage to qualify for

post-election federal campaign funds. He also could take

some consolation from the fact that his efforts reduced ballot

access restrictions for future third-party and independent

candidates. If John Anderson failed to go out with a bang, he

at least achieved something more than a whimper.

PRIMARY SOURCES

588.   Anderson, John B. "Developing a 'Grand Coalition.'"
        Party Coalitions in the 1980's, pp. 371-78. Edited
        by Seymour M. Lipset. San Francisco: Institute for
        Contemporary Studies, 1981. 489 pp. (item 69)

        Anderson explores possibility of several new coali-
tions combining forces to change traditional bi-partisan
alignment; examples based on groups dissatisfied with Reagan
administration.

589.   "Transcript of Campaign's First Presidential Debate,
        with Reagan vs. Anderson." New York Times 22, Septem-
        ber 1980, sec. 2, p. 6.

        Candidates' responses to panelists' queries on domes-
tic issues.

590.   "Transcript of Statement by Anderson." New York Times
        5 (November 1980), p. 21.

        Text of Anderson's concession speech.

SECONDARY SOURCES

591.   Abramson, Paul R., John H. Aldrich, and David W. Rhode.
       Change and Continuity in the 1980 Elections. Washing-
       ton, D.C.: Congressional Quarterly Press, 1982, pp.
       172-183.

       Extensive analysis of survey data including section
on Anderson supporters and how his campaign compared to other
independent presidential campaigns.

592.   Alpern, David M. "A Voice in the Wilderness." News-
       week 96 (3 November 1980): 37.

       A review of Anderson's impact on 1980 election and
future ones.

593.   American Enterprise Institute for Public Policy
       Research. The Candidates 1980: Where They Stand.
       Washington, D.C.: American Enterprise Institute
       for Public Policy Research, 1980. 72 pp.

       Anderson's position on key campaign issues.

594.   Balz, Dan. "Anderson." Pursuit of the Presidency,
       1980. Edited by Richard Harwood. New York: Putnam's,
       1980, pp. 207-31.

       Concentrating on early stages of campaign, chapter
traces evolution of Anderson's liberalism.

595.   "The Basic Speech: John B. Anderson." New York Times
       4, March 1980, sec. 2, p. 8.

       Stock campaign speech containing heart of Anderson's
message to voters.

596.   Bisnow, Mark. Diary of a Dark Horse: The 1980 Anderson
       Presidential Campaign. Carbondale, Ill.: Southern
       Illinois University Press, 1983. 329 pp.

       The best existing source for information on the
Anderson campaign. Written by Anderson's press secretary,
this is an insider's account.

597.   Bonafede, Dom. "Can Anderson Succeed Where Teddy
        Roosevelt Failed?" National Journal 12 (17 May 1980):
        806-10.

        In-depth look at Anderson campaign organization's
efforts to make him a serious contender.

598.   Bressler, Robert J. "1980 and 1964: A Perspective on
        the Anderson Candidacy." USA Today 109 (July 1980):
        6-7.

        Anderson's appeal to moderates could move political
dialogue back towards center and force controversial issues
into debate forum.

599.   Cook, Rhodes. "Anderson: Running on the GOP Left."
        Congressional Quarterly Weekly Report 37 (3 November
        1979): 2467-70.

        Survey of Anderson's congressional career and his bid
for GOP nomination.

600.   Drew, Elizabeth. Portrait of An Election, the 1980
        Presidential Campaign. New York: Simon and Schuster,
        1981.

        Contains items 601 and 602.

601.   _____. "Reporter at Large. 1980: Anderson." New
        Yorker 56 (12 May 1980): 48-50+.

        Anderson offers reasons, justification for indepen-
dent candidacy. Included in item 600.

602.   _____. "Reporter at Large. 1980: Anderson." New
        Yorker 56 (13 October 1980): 150+.

        Traces evolution of Anderson candidacy detailing
campaign's unique problems and strategies. Included in item
600.

603.   Germond, Jack, and Jules Witcover, eds. "Anderson and
        the 'Alienated Middle.'" Blue Smoke and Mirrors:
        How Reagan Won and Why Carter Lost the Election of
        1980. New York: Viking Press, 1981, pp. 228-42.

        Authors analyze difficulty of Anderson campaign
running without major party organization and backing.

604.   Golubovskis, George M. Crazy Dreaming: The Anderson
        Campaign, 1980. Flint, Mich.: Talking Seal Press,
        1981. 123 pp.

        Unique account of campaign by Anderson volunteer in
Michigan.

605.   Hoffman, Nicholas von. "The Third Man Theme." New
        York Times 28, September 1980, sec. 4, p. 97.

        Historical account of third parties with Anderson
campaign viewed in context.

606.   Johnson, Donald B., comp. National Party Platforms,
        1840-1976. Supplement 1980. Urbana, Ill.: Univer-
        sity of Illinois Press, 1982. 233 pp.

        Includes National Unity Campaign platform. Supple-
ments item 3.

607.   Judis, John. "An Anderson Difference?" Progressive
        44 (November 1980: 48-50.

        Anderson's potential effect on presidential election
more impressive than his platform.

608.   McCarthy, Eugene. "Anderson's Way Will Not Be Easy."
        Wall Street Journal 22, April 1980, p. 24.

        Author warns of set-backs built into two-party system
that independent candidates must overcome. Interesting primarily because of McCarthy's third-party background.

609.   Masters, Roger. "John Anderson: A New Coalition."
        Wall Street Journal, 18 March 1980, p. 24.

        Author suggests political realignment and new coali-
tions may result in support for Anderson.

610.   Moore, Jonathan, ed. The Campaign for President: 1980
        in Retrospect. Cambridge, Mass.: Ballinger Publish-
        ing, 1981. 304 pp.

        Anderson and key decision-making staff from various
campaigns evaluate 1980 campaign.

611.   "Presidential Trial Heats, 1936–1980." Gallup Opinion
        Index 183 (December 1980): 13.

        How Anderson polls in three-way contest from March
to October.

612.   Ranney, Austin, ed. The American Elections of 1980.
        Washington, D.C.: American Enterprise Institute for
        Public Policy Research, 1980. 391 pp.

        Collection of essays on all aspects of 1980 national
elections, including excellent and numerous graphics comparing
Anderson's Republican and independent campaigns to other con-
tenders.'

613.   Schwartz, Tony. "The Anderson Principle." New York
        Times 17, February 1980, sec. 4, p. 35+.

        Lengthy review of Anderson's political and personal
background, plus his campaign for Republican nomination.

614.   Shapiro, W. "John Anderson: The Nice Guy Syndrome."
        Atlantic 245 (February 1980): 4+.

        Frustrations of a qualified, experienced candidate
with little chance of winning.

*   Smallwood, Frank. The Other Candidates: Third Parties
        in Presidential Elections (item 105).

        December 1981 interview discusses accomplishments of
presidential campaign and possibility of third-party bid in
1984.

615.   Smith, Paul A. Electing a President: Information and
        Control. New York: Praeger, 1982, pp. 139–44, 181–
        92.

        Emphasizes mechanics, strategy, and organization of
Anderson campaign, compared and contrasted to national parties'
campaigns.

616.   Stacks, John F. "Squeezed Out of the Middle." Time 116
        (17 November 1980): 52.

        Reflections on campaign's shortcomings and failures.

617. _____ . Watershed, the Campaign for the Presidency,
        1980. New York: Times Books, 1981, pp. 159-74, 218-
        24.

        Anderson, potential antithesis to Vietnam War-Watergate
era leader, unable to remain distinctively different and truly
moderate throughout campaign.

618. Sulzberger, A.D., Jr. "On the Issues: John B. Ander-
        son." New York Times 29, March 1980, p. 9.

        Anderson's position on foreign and domestic affairs
contrasted with other Republican candidates.'

619. "Symposium: The Anderson Candidacy." Nation 230 (17
        May 1980): 582-87.

        Staff members and affiliates of journal submit opin-
ions on Anderson, and most agree he is unsuitable alternative.

AUTHOR INDEX

Aaron, Daniel, 309, 470
Aberbach, Joel D., 368
Abney, F. Glenn, 404
Abrams, Richard M., 471
Abramson, Paul R., 591
Ader, Emile B., 369
Agar, Herbert, 11
Aherns, Gary, 12
Aldrich, John H., 591
Alexander, Herbert E., 13, 370, 576
Alfred, Helen, 182
Allen, Emory A., 122, 123
Alpern, David M., 592
Alperovitz, Gar, 191
American Enterprise Institute for Public Policy Research, 593
Anderson, John B., 588
Aptheker, Herbert, 310
Argersinger, Peter H., 153
Armstrong, Forrest H., 371
Arnett, Alex Matthews, 154
Ashbaugh, Carolyn, 280
Ashby, LeRoy, 472
Bacciocco, Edward J., 356
Bain, Chester W., 372
Baldwin, C.B., 528
Balz, Dan, 594
Baritz, Loren, 183
Barnard, William D., 373
Barnes, Jack, 344, 345
Bartley, Numan V., 374, 375
Bass, Jack, 376
Bates, James L., 473
Bedford, Henry F., 249
Behr, Roy L., 96

Bell, Daniel, 193, 194, 377, 378
Bell, Leslie, 14
Bellamy, Edward, 124
Bennett, David H., 556
Bennett, James D., 15
Bennett, Stephen E., 430
Berenson, William M., 379
Berman, William C., 380
Bernd, Joseph L., 381
Best, James J., 451
Best, Judith V., 16
Bibbee, M. Jane, 34
Bickel, Alexander M., 17
Billington, Monroe L., 382
Billington, Ray A., 18
Binkley, Wilfred E., 19
Birdsall, Stephen S., 383
Bisnow, Mark, 596
Black, Earl, 384, 385, 386
Black, Merle, 386
Blackorby, Edward C., 557
Blocker, Jack S., Jr., 547
Blum, John Morton, 474, 475
Bode, Ken, 577, 578
Bonafede, Dom, 597
Bond, Robert D., 379
Bone, Hugh A., 20, 21, 121
Boorstin, Daniel J., 22
Boughan, Karl M., 387
Bowers, Claude G., 476
Boyd, Richard W., 388
Brandt, Joseph, 338
Braun, Alan G., 70
Breitman, George, 345, 346
Bressler, Robert J., 598
Brinkley, Alan, 558

Jodgson, Godfrey, 391
Johnpoll, Bernard K., 209, 259
Johnpoll, Lillian, 209
Johnson, Donald B., 3, 606
Johnson, Lyndon B., 362
Johnson, Oakley C., 210, 238, 241, 322
Jones, Bill, 416
Jones, Melvin E., 419
Jones, Rochelle, 583
Judis, John, 569, 607
Kampelman, Max, 323
Kazin, Alfred, 188
Keeran, Roger, 324
Kehde, Ned, 232
Keller, Morton, 494
Kempton, Murray, 325
Kendall, Willmoore, 90
Kennedy, David M., 495
Key, V.O., Jr., 59, 417
Killian, Lewis M., 418
King, S.S., 140
Kirby, Jack T., 496
Kirkpatrick, Samuel A., 419
Klehr, Harvey, 326
Kleppner, Paul, 60
Kobler, John, 552
Kolko, Gabriel, 497
Kornhauser, William, 61
Kraditor, Aileen S., 211
Kramer, Dale, 62
Kreuter, Gretchen, 260
Kreuter, Kent, 260
Lachicotte, Alberta, 420
Ladd, Everett C., Jr., 63, 64
Lader, Lawrence, 212
LaFollette, Belle, 522
LaFollette, Fola, 522
LaFollette, Robert, 518
Landau, Saul, 358
Larson, Robert, 164
Lasch, Christopher, 65
Laslett, John, 213, 214
Lazarus, Edward H., 96
Lease, Mary Elizabeth, 141
Lederman, Susan S., 87
Lehnen, Robert G., 421

Lemmon, Sarah M., 422
Lens, Sidney, 189, 215
Lerner, Michael, 190
Levenstein, Harvey A., 327
Levin, Nora, 216
Liebman, Arthur, 217
Lieske, Joel A., 423
Link, Arthur S., 498, 523
Lipset, Seymour M., 66, 67, 68, 69, 84, 214, 424
Lloyd, Henry Demarest, 142, 143, 144
Long, Priscilla, 355
Longley, Lawrence D., 70, 82
Lord, Russell, 537
Loucks, Henry L., 145
Lowitt, Richard, 499
Lubell, Samuel, 425
Luce, Phillip A., 359
Lynd, Straughton, 191
Lyons, Paul, 328
MacBride, Roger L., 570
McCarthy, Eugene, 574, 575, 608
McConnell, Grant, 71
McCormick, Richard P., 72
McCoy, Donald R., 562
MacDonald, Dwight, 538
McDonnell, Richard A., 426
MacDougall, Curtis D., 539
McEvoy, James, III, 427, 428
MacKay, Kenneth C., 524
McKean, Dayton,D., 73
McMath, Robert C., 165
McMurray, Donald L., 166
McRae, Duncan, Jr., 74
Macy, Jesse, 75
Mahood, H.R., 454
Malkin, Maurice L., 301
Maney, Patrick J., 525
Mann, Arthur, 500
Marcus, Sheldon, 563
Markowitz, Norman D., 540
Marsh, Margaret S., 284
Martin, Boyd A., 399
Martin, James M., 285
Martin, Roscoe C., 167
Masters, Roger, 609

TITLE INDEX

Age of Reform: From Bryan to
  FDR, The, 54
Aggregation Effects in the
  Ecological Study of Pres-
  idential Voting, 453
Agony of the American Left,
  The, 65
Agrarian Crusade, A Chroni-
  cle of the Farmer in
  Politics, The, 554
Alabama: Transition and
  Alienation, 449
Alienation and Political
  Behavior, 368
Aliens and Dissenters:
  Federal Suppression of
  Radicals, 1903-1933, 220
Alternative Vision: The
  Socialist Party in the
  1930's, An, 248
Ambiguous Legacy: The Left
  in American Politics,
  226
America Votes: A Handbook
  of Contemporary American
  Election Statistics, 7
American as Anarchist:
  Reflections on Indigenous
  Radicalism, The, 281
American Century: The
  Recollections of Bertha
  W. Howe, 1866-1966, An,
  241
American Commissar, 305
American Communism and
  Soviet Russia: The For-
  mative Period, 311

American Communism in Crisis,
  1943-1957, 304
American Communist Party: A
  Critical History, 1919-1957,
  The, 318
American Dissenter: The Life
  of Algie Martin Simons,
  1870-1950, An, 260
American Elections of 1980,
  The, 612
American Farmers' Movements,
  102
American Left in the Twentieth
  Century, The, 200
American Left, 1955-1970: A
  National Union Catalog of
  Pamphlets Published in the
  United States and Canada,
  The, 232
American Left: Radical Poli-
  tical Thought in the Twen-
  tieth Century, The, 183
American Melodrama: The Presi-
  dential Campaign of 1968,
  An, 391
American Party System: An Intro-
  duction to the Study of Poli-
  tical Parties in the United
  States, The, 78
American Party System: Conclu-
  ding Observations, The, 68
American People's Money, The
  128
American Political Parties: A
  Selective Guide to Parties
  and Movements of the Twen-
  tieth Century, 10

161

DATE DUE

11 02 '88	
MAR 0 8 '89	
FEB 13 '91	
APR 4 1997	

BRODART, INC.   Cat. No. 23-221